D1400465

The Nature of Matter

Theme: Scale

THINK
LIKE A SCIENTIST

BERRY, BERRY COLD

Have you ever seen a tree or a bush after an ice storm? If so, it may have looked something like the tree in the photo. The day before the photo was taken, the branches and berries were dry. During the night, rain covered the tree with water. Then a drop in the air temperature caused the water to lose heat. The result is ice-encrusted berries. Scientists study such changes in water and in other kinds of matter. They also study how energy is related to these changes.

THINK LIKE A SCIENTIST

Questioning In this unit you'll study how changes in energy are related to changes in state, such as freezing and melting. You'll investigate questions such as these.
- How Does Energy Affect Matter?
- How Can Matter Change?

Observing, Testing, Hypothesizing In the Activity "Cooling Race," you'll compare the cooling rates of water mixed with ice cubes and water mixed with crushed ice. You'll hypothesize what happens to heat energy in the water as it cools.

Researching In the Resource "Particle Energy," you'll learn about the relationship between temperature, heat, and the energy of particles that make up matter. You'll also find out how this energy is involved in changes in state.

Drawing Conclusions After you've completed your investigations, you'll draw conclusions about what you've learned—and get new ideas.

CHAPTER 1

CHARACTERISTICS OF MATTER

When you take ice cubes from the freezer of your refrigerator, you are removing solid chunks of water. Yesterday, you put liquid water in the ice-cube trays. Besides becoming cold and solid, how else has the water changed? Have the mass, density, and volume of the water been affected?

PEOPLE USING SCIENCE

Glaciologist Erik Blake surveys the bleak, white landscape around him. As a glaciologist (glā shē äl′ ə-jist), or scientist who studies glaciers, he is exploring Hubbard Glacier in Canada's rugged Yukon Territory.

A glacier is a giant mass of ice that moves slowly over land. The Hubbard Glacier, which is 140 km (87 mi) long, is among the largest in North America. The glacier is a natural laboratory for Blake. He seeks to understand how it moves and the kinds of wildlife found in this harsh environment. By studying ice cores taken from deep in the glacier, he can learn what conditions were like thousands of years ago, when the ice formed.

Where a glacier meets the ocean, great mountains of ice break off and fall into the sea. Yet these massive ice mountains float! What questions would you like to ask about how glacial ice differs from liquid water?

Coming Up

◀ Erik Blake, glaciologist

HOW CAN YOU DESCRIBE MATTER?

Suppose you were asked to compare a brick and a basketball. List the characteristics you would use to describe each object. Could another person identify both objects based on your lists?

Activity

A Matter of Mass

A golf ball and a table-tennis ball are about the same size. Which contains more matter? How can you measure the amount of matter in an object?

MATERIALS
- 3 sealed containers, labeled *A*, *B*, and *C*
- balance and masses
- *Science Notebook*

Procedure

1. Look at the three containers your teacher will provide. Without picking them up, **compare** their sizes and shapes. **Record** your observations in your *Science Notebook*.

2. Now pick up each container, but don't shake it. Based on the way the containers feel, arrange them in order from heaviest to lightest.

3. **Make a chart** like the one shown.

4. Using a balance, **measure** in grams the **mass**—the amount of matter—of each container. **Record** the results in your chart.

Container	Mass (g)	Contents
A		
B		
C		

Step 2

See **SCIENCE** and **MATH TOOLBOX** page *H9 if you need to review Using a Balance.*

Step 4

5. One container is filled with sand, one with water, and one with cotton. Based on your observations, infer which material is in each container. In the *Contents* column of your chart, record your inferences. Then open each container and check your inferences.

Analyze and Conclude

1. By studying and handling the containers, what can you infer about the amount of space taken up by each of the materials?

2. What did you learn about the amount of matter in each container? How did you learn this?

3. Describe what you learned about mass and matter by doing this activity.

Science in Literature

CAN ICE SINK?

"Place an ice cube in a glass of water. Why do you think it floats? . . . Now add an ice cube to half a glass of alcohol. Why do you think the ice sinks?

An ice cube will float in cooking oil, but just barely. It's beautiful to see because the melting ice forms giant drops of water that flow ever so slowly through the clear, thick oil. It's like watching rain drops falling in slow motion."

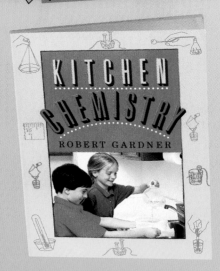

Kitchen Chemistry
by Robert Gardner
Julian Messner, 1988

Read *Kitchen Chemistry* by Robert Gardner to find out how to complete this experiment and for other experiments that will help you explore the nature of matter on your own.

Activity

A Matter of Space

Does a softball take up more space than a shoe? Try to describe the amount of space each of these objects takes up. Does the amount of matter an object contains affect how much space it takes up?

Procedure

1. If you place some cotton in one container and an equal mass of sand in another container, **predict** which material will take up more space.

2. Fill a plastic bag with cotton balls. Put as much cotton as you can in the bag without squashing it down.

3. Use a balance to **measure** the mass of the cotton. **Record** this measurement in your *Science Notebook*.

4. Remove the bag of cotton from the balance. Place another plastic bag on the empty balance pan. Add sand to the bag until it has the same mass as the bag of cotton.

5. Pour the sand from the plastic bag into a measuring cup. **Measure** and **record** how many milliliters of sand were in the bag. Then pour the sand back into its original container.

Step 5

See **SCIENCE** and **MATH TOOLBOX** page H7 if you need to review **Measuring Volume.**

6. Take the cotton balls from the bag and push them down into the measuring cup. **Record** how many milliliters of cotton you have. You may have to fill the measuring cup more than once.

Analyze and Conclude

1. Which bag contained more mass, the bag of cotton or the bag of sand?

2. Which material took up more space, the cotton or the sand?

3. Can an object's volume be determined just from its mass? Explain your answer.

Activity
Checking for Purity

The sphere and cube are about the same size. One is made of clay; the other is a mixture of clay and some lighter material. How can you tell which is which?

MATERIALS
- clay cube
- clay ball
- balance and masses
- metric measuring cup
- water
- *Science Notebook*

- -

Procedure

1. Study a clay ball and a clay cube carefully. You may handle them, but do not change either object's shape or size. **Make inferences** about the mass and volume of each object and **record** your inferences in your *Science Notebook*.

 Math Hint *Record your inferences using the >, <, or = symbols.*

Step 1

2. **Measure** and **record** the mass of each object.

3. Half fill a measuring cup with water. **Record** the volume of the water in milliliters.

4. Carefully place the ball in the measuring cup. **Observe** what happens to the water level. **Record** the new volume reading. **Calculate** the volume of the ball. Then remove the ball, shaking any excess water into the measuring cup.

5. Repeat step 4 with the cube.

Analyze and Conclude

1. What did you **infer** about the mass and volume of the two objects in step 1?

2. How did the masses of the ball and cube compare?

3. What did the changing water level in the measuring cup tell you about each object?

4. **Hypothesize** which object is made of pure clay and which is made of clay and some lighter material. Give evidence to support your hypothesis.

Measuring Mass and Volume

Reading Focus How can you find the mass and volume of an object?

▲ **Which package would you rather be holding?**

It's a cold day, and you and a friend are standing at a bus stop. You've been shopping, and you each have a package to hold. One package is quite heavy; the other is lighter but is larger and more bulky. Which package would you choose to hold?

Like everything around you, the packages are made up of matter. **Matter** is anything that has mass and volume. In fact, the problem of which package is easier to hold involves these two physical properties—mass and volume. As seen in the activities on pages C6 to C8, these properties can be measured. To review and practice your skills for measuring these and other properties, read pages H6 to H9 in the Science and Math Toolbox.

Mass

The heaviness of each package is directly related to its mass. **Mass** is a measure of how much matter something contains. Weight is a measure of the force of gravity acting on a mass. So the more matter an object contains—the greater its mass—the more it will weigh.

When you weigh yourself on a bathroom scale, the scale measures the effect of Earth's gravitational force on the mass of your body. So how could you find the mass of your body? You would have to compare the unknown mass of your body to some known mass. For example, you could sit on one end of a seesaw and have someone add objects of known mass to the other end. When the seesaw

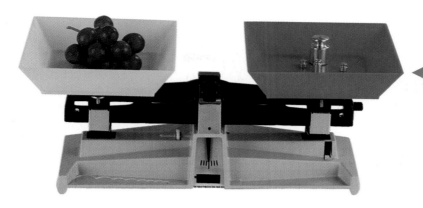

Finding the Mass of an Object
The mass of an object is found by placing the object in one pan of a balance and objects of known masses in the other.

balanced, you'd know that your mass was the same as the total mass of the objects. Now you can see why the instrument used to measure the mass of an object is called a balance.

The most common metric units used to measure mass are grams (g) and kilograms (kg). A penny has a mass of about 2 g. A kilogram is one thousand times the mass of a gram. A large cantaloupe has a mass of about 1 kg.

Other units are also used for measuring mass in the metric system. For example, the mass of a very light object could be measured in milligrams (mg). One milligram is equal to one thousandth $(\frac{1}{1000})$ of a gram.

Volume

The **volume** of an object is the amount of space it takes up. For example, an inflated balloon takes up more space—has greater volume—than an empty balloon. Volume can also be used to express *capacity*—that is, how much material something can hold. A swimming pool can hold a lot more water than a teacup can.

The basic unit of volume in the metric system is the cubic meter (m^3). But because 1 m^3 is such a large amount, the liter (L) is more commonly used. A liter (lēt'ər) is slightly larger than a quart. Many

soft drinks are sold in 2-L containers. Units used to measure smaller volumes include the centiliter (cL), which is one hundredth of a liter, and the milliliter (mL), which is one thousandth of a liter.

An instrument called a graduated cylinder, or graduate, is used to measure liquid volumes. Using a graduate is similar to using a measuring cup.

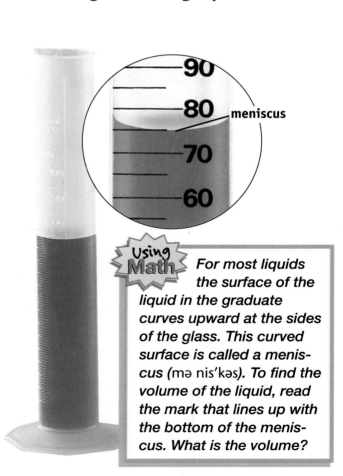

meniscus

Using Math
For most liquids the surface of the liquid in the graduate curves upward at the sides of the glass. This curved surface is called a meniscus (mə nis'kəs). To find the volume of the liquid, read the mark that lines up with the bottom of the meniscus. What is the volume?

Suppose you want to know how much water or some other liquid is in a container of some kind. First you pour the liquid from the container into a graduate. Then you measure the level of the liquid against the scale marked on the side of the graduate. Graduates come in many sizes. This makes it possible for you to measure small volumes, large volumes, and all volumes in between.

There are two methods for finding the volume of a solid. One method is used for finding volumes of solids that have regular geometric shapes, such as cubes, spheres, and rectangular blocks. For any solid with a regular shape, you can measure such dimensions as length, width, height, and diameter. Then you can calculate the volume of the solid by substituting the measurements in a mathematical formula. For example, the volume of a rectangular block can be found by multiplying its length times its width times its height. The formula for this calculation is below.

$$V = l \times w \times h$$

Many solids do not have a regular shape. A rock, for example, is likely to have an irregular shape. The volume of these kinds of solids can be found by using the water displacement method.

Suppose you want to use the water displacement method to find the volume of a rock, such as the one shown in the picture. The first step is to find a graduate large enough to hold the rock. Next, you fill the graduate about one-third full with water. Then you lower the rock into the graduate, as shown. ■

Internet Field Trip

Visit **www.eduplace.com** to find out more about measurement.

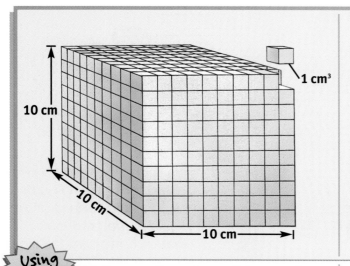

10 cm

10 cm

10 cm

1 cm³

Using Math *Volumes of regular solids are often expressed in cubic centimeters (cm³). A cubic centimeter is the volume of a cube 1 cm long on each edge. One cm³ is equal to 1 mL. What is the volume of this regular solid?*

The volume of water in the graduate is 30 mL. When the object being measured is lowered into the water, the water level rises to 45 mL. What is the volume of the object?

Density

Imagine yourself in this situation. You have just packed and sealed two identical boxes. One box contains a down pillow, and the other box contains books. The problem is, you have forgotten which box contains which item. Since the two boxes look exactly alike, how can you solve this problem without opening one of the boxes?

You can probably think of an easy solution. All you have to do is pick up each box. The box containing books will be much heavier than the one containing the pillow.

Density

You solved your problem by comparing the masses of two objects (cartons) having equal volumes. You may not have realized it, but you used a very important property of matter—density—to solve your problem.

Density refers to the amount of matter packed into a given space. In other words, **density** is the amount of mass in a certain volume of matter. To get an idea of what density is, look at the objects on the balance shown in the photograph below.

What will happen if the block on the left is replaced with another block made of the same stuff, but equal in size (volume) to the block on the right? The balance will tilt to the left. The block on the left has the greater density.

You can calculate the density of any sample of matter if you know two things—its mass and its volume. You can find the density of the sample by dividing its mass by its volume. The formula for finding density is below.

$$D = m/v$$

For example, suppose you are working with a piece of metal that has a volume of 2.0 mL and a mass of 9.0 g. By using the formula, you can determine the density of that metal. Notice that density measurements always include mass and volume units.

$$D = 9.0 \text{ g}/2.0 \text{ mL} = 4.5 \text{ g/mL}$$

Understanding Density
Since the two blocks balance each other, they must have the same mass. But the block on the left is obviously smaller than the one on the right—its volume is less. Thus the block on the left has a greater density than the block on the right. ▶

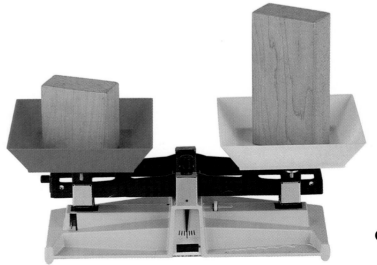

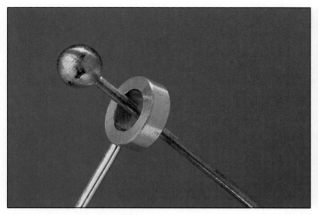 

The ball and ring are both made of brass. When they are at the same temperature (*left*), the ball fits easily through the ring. How does heating the ball affect its volume (*right*)?

Using Density to Identify Materials

Density is a characteristic property of all matter. This means that a particular kind of matter always has the same density, regardless of where the matter comes from or where it is measured. For example, the density of pure water is 1.0 g/mL. This means that a milliliter of water has a mass of 1 g. The table below gives the densities of some common materials.

Since every substance has a definite density, this property can be used to identify materials. For example, suppose you measure the mass and volume of an object and find its density is 7.9 g/mL. Could you make a reasonable guess as to what material the object is made of? You could if you had a table of densities like the one on this page. Use the table to find what the object is most likely made of.

Density and Temperature

Notice that the table lists the densities of the materials at a particular temperature—in this case, 20°C. This is done because temperature affects density. As a general rule, matter expands when it gains heat and contracts when it loses heat. In other words, the volume of a material increases as its temperature goes up and decreases as its temperature goes down.

How does a change in volume affect density? Look again at the formula for density: $D = m/v$. If the mass of a material doesn't change and the volume of the material increases, its density

Densities of Some Common Materials at 20°C			
Material	**Density (g/mL)**	**Material**	**Density (g/mL)**
gold	19.3	water	1.0
lead	11.3	oil	0.90
silver	10.5	wood (oak)	0.7
copper	8.9	wood (pine)	0.4
iron	7.9	oxygen	0.0014
aluminum	2.7	helium	0.0002

decreases. On the other hand, if the volume of a material decreases and its mass stays the same, its density increases. How does heating the ball shown on page C14 change its density?

Float or Sink?

Density can be useful in predicting whether an object will sink or float in water. The density of water is 1.0 g/mL. Any material with a density less than 1.0 g/mL will float in water. Anything with a density greater than 1.0 g/mL will sink. How might such information be useful?

Imagine you're going to boil some eggs for breakfast. You want to make sure the eggs aren't spoiled. The density of a fresh egg is about 1.2 g/mL. The density of a spoiled egg is about 0.9 g/mL. If you

place an egg in water and it floats, what does this tell you about the egg?

Density in Calculations

Density can also be used to answer questions about the purity of a material. Suppose you have a chunk of metal with a volume of 10 mL. You're told that the metal is pure silver. How could you find out for sure?

You could start by looking up the density of silver, which is 10.5 g/mL. This tells you that 1 mL of silver has a mass of 10.5 g. So 10 mL of pure silver will have a mass of 10×10.5 g, or 105 g. Now all you have to do is measure the mass of your chunk of metal. ■

Technology Link
CD-ROM

INVESTIGATE FURTHER!

Use the **Science Processor CD-ROM**, *The Nature of Matter* (Investigation 1, Good as Gold) to travel to San Francisco during the 1849 gold rush. While there, decide whether a miner is trying to sell you real gold or fool's gold.

INVESTIGATION 1 WRAP-UP

REVIEW

1. Define *mass*, *volume*, and *density*.

2. How can you find the volume of a cube and of an irregularly shaped object?

CRITICAL THINKING

3. When might you want to find the density of an object?

4. Suppose you have a 10-g cube that floats in water and a 10-g sphere that does not. What can you infer about the volume of each object? Why?

INVESTIGATION 2

WHAT MAKES UP MATTER?

Think about what happens when water is spilled on a kitchen countertop. If you wipe the countertop with a dry sponge, where does the water go? How is the sponge different from the countertop? In this investigation you'll find out how the particles that make up matter give matter its properties.

Activity

Always Room for More

When you add sugar to a glass of iced tea, where does the sugar go? How does the sugar "fit" into the full glass?

MATERIALS

- goggles
- 2 plastic cups
- marbles
- spoon
- sand
- water
- sugar
- *Science Notebook*

SAFETY

Wear goggles during this activity.

Procedure

1. Fill a cup to the brim with marbles. **Infer** whether the cup is full or whether there is room for more matter. **Record** your inference in your *Science Notebook*.

2. Using a spoon, carefully add sand to the cup. Gently tap the sides of the cup as you add the sand. Continue until no more sand will fit in the cup. **Make an inference** about the space in the cup now.

3. Slowly and carefully pour water into the cup until no more water can be added.

4. Fill a second cup with water. Carefully add a spoonful of sugar and stir. **Record** your observations.

Step 1

Step 3

Step 4

Analyze and Conclude

1. Was any matter in the cup before you added the marbles? If so, what happened to it?

2. Why could the cup full of marbles still hold sand and water?

3. How would this activity have been different if you had started by filling the cup with water?

4. Use your observations of the first cup to **infer** what happened to the sugar that was added to the second cup. How does the sugar "fit" in the water?

5. **Make a sketch** of what you think the mixture of sugar and water would look like if you could see how the two materials fit together.

Technology Link
CD-ROM

INVESTIGATE FURTHER!

Use the **Science Processor CD-ROM**, *The Nature of Matter* (Unit Opening Investigation, What's the Matter?) to compare the characteristics of liquids, solids, and gases.

Activity

Racing Liquids

A paper towel soaks up water. Do other types of paper do the same? Paper strips can help you model how particles are packed in different materials.

Procedure

1. Cut a strip 2.5 cm wide and 15 cm long from each kind of paper in the Materials list. Cut one end of each strip to form a point.

 See **SCIENCE** *and* **MATH TOOLBOX** page H6 if you need to review *Using a Tape Measure or Ruler.*

2. Study dry samples of each kind of paper with a hand lens. In your *Science Notebook*, **describe** how they are different. **Predict** which paper strip water will move through most quickly.

3. Tape the strips to the bottom of a coat hanger so that the points of the tips hang the same distance below the hanger.

4. Pour water into a pan and add a few drops of food coloring to the water. Hold the coat hanger above the pan so that the tips of the paper strips touch the water.

5. **Observe** as the water "races" up the strips. When the water reaches the top of one strip, remove the hanger. Then lay all five strips of paper on a flat surface.

Step 4

Analyze and Conclude

1. Using the distances that water traveled through the strips, **list** the types of paper in order from fastest to slowest.

2. Imagine that you could observe the water and paper through an extremely high powered microscope. **Make a sketch** showing how you think the water moves through the paper.

3. Do samples of matter contain "empty" spaces? **Give evidence** to support your conclusion.

Structure of Matter

Reading Focus What are some effects of the motion of particles of matter?

▲ **Even in still air, specks of dust dance and dart about.**

Picture yourself sitting in your room on a quiet summer afternoon. You're home alone, there's nothing to do, and you're *bored*! You're so bored that you begin staring at the specks of dust dancing in a sparkling beam of sunlight. Even with all the doors and windows closed and no hint of a breeze, you notice that the tiny specks dart about as if they were being stirred by an invisible hand. What could be moving the dust around?

Particles in Motion

The moving specks of dust offer evidence of the structure and nature of matter. Matter is composed of very tiny particles that are constantly in motion. The particles that make up matter are much smaller than the tiniest speck of dust. These particles are so small, in fact, that they can't be seen, even with the best microscope your school owns.

Air is made up of such particles, moving through space. As the particles of air move about, they collide with each other and with everything in your room, including the specks of dust. The movements of dust specks are caused by particles of air bouncing the specks of dust around!

It's easy to see the effects of moving air particles. Inflated objects, such as balloons and basketballs, provide evidence that air is made up of particles. When you put air into a container, the moving air particles continuously bang against the sides of the container. It's these collisions that keep objects inflated.

Air, of course, is a gas. Actually it's a mixture of several different gases. Because gases are invisible, it's easy to think of them as being made up of tiny

Evidence for Particle Motion

▲ A colored liquid being added to water

▲ The mixture 5 minutes later

▲ The mixture after an additional 10 minutes

moving particles. But what about other forms of matter? What evidence do we have that liquids and solids are made up of moving particles? Look at the pictures on this page.

❶ Like still air in a room, the water in the jar seems calm. Yet the water and the colored liquid mix together on their own. This mixing indicates that liquids, like gases, are made up of moving particles.

❷ As the particles of water and colored liquid bump into each other, the particles spread out and mixing occurs.

❸ If left to stand, the particles of colored liquid and water continue to move until they are evenly mixed together.

So evidence indicates that gases and liquids are made up of tiny moving particles. What about solids? It's hard to visualize something as hard and unchanging as a rock or your desk being made up of moving particles. But it's true! You'll find out about evidence that supports this idea as you read on.

States of Matter

Think about some kinds of matter that you see every day, such as air, water, ice, iron, wood, syrup, sugar, and cloth. As different as these materials are, they can all be classified into one of three major categories, or states. The three common **states of matter** are solid, liquid, and gas. Study the drawings and descriptions of these states on page C21.

As you have just read, solids, liquids, and gases are all made up of tiny particles in constant motion. The particles that make up a substance are attracted to each other to some degree. The state in which a substance is found depends on two things: how fast the particles are moving and how strongly the particles are attracted to each other.

The forces of attraction among particles are different for different substances. For example, particles of helium gas barely attract each other at all. These particles fly around even when they are moving at fairly slow speeds.

Particles of water have slightly stronger attractions to each other. These particles have to be moving at a pretty good speed before they actually separate and fly around. The chemical forces between particles of iron are very strong. These particles have to be moving at very high speeds before they overcome the forces of attraction and fly around.

The state in which a substance is found depends on the nature of its particles and the speed at which they are moving. As you will discover, the motion of the particles can be changed. ■

States of Matter

SOLIDS
In a solid, chemical forces hold the particles in place. The particles vibrate back and forth but don't leave their positions. This is why a solid keeps its shape.

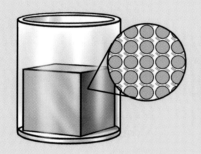

LIQUIDS
In a liquid, particles move faster and farther apart than particles in a solid. The particles in a liquid can slip and slide past each other. This is why a liquid has no definite shape.

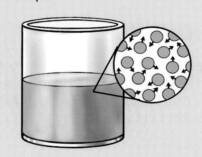

GASES
In a gas, particles move so fast that chemical forces can't hold them together. This is why particles in a gas spread out to fill their container and why gas has no definite shape or volume.

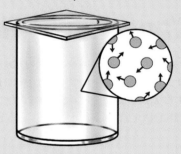

INVESTIGATION 2 WRAP-UP

REVIEW

1. What is matter made of?

2. Why do solids have a definite shape but liquids and gases do not?

CRITICAL THINKING

3. Iron expands when it is heated. Draw a sketch of how the particles of a piece of iron might look at 10°C and at 50°C.

4. If you add 2 mL of sugar to 100 mL of water, the volume of the water does not change. What do you think will happen if you keep adding more and more sugar? Why?

HOW DOES ENERGY AFFECT MATTER?

What happens when you put some hard kernels of corn in a pan, hold the pan over a fire, and shake it? A few minutes later you have popcorn! In this investigation you'll find out how energy changes matter in different ways.

Activity

Cooling Race

Suppose you are enjoying a glass of lemonade on a hot day. What happens to your drink when you add ice cubes? How do the ice cubes change? Can these changes be described in terms of energy?

Procedure

1. **Make a chart** in your *Science Notebook* like the one below.

2. Half fill two plastic cups with water. Put a thermometer in each cup. **Record** the water temperature under *Start* in your chart.

Water Temperature						
	Start	**3 min**	**6 min**	**9 min**	**12 min**	**15 min**
Water + Ice Cubes						
Water + Crushed Ice						

Step 3

3. Put two ice cubes in a plastic bag and set them on one pan of a balance. Place a second bag on the other pan. Use a spoon to add crushed ice to this bag until the pans balance.

4. Add the ice cubes to one cup and the crushed ice to the other cup.

5. At three-minute intervals, **measure** the temperature of the water in each cup. **Record** each measurement in your chart. Continue for 15 minutes.

6. **Make a line graph** that shows how the temperature of the ice-water mixtures changed over time. Use a different color for each line on your graph.

 See **SCIENCE** and **MATH TOOLBOX** page H13 if you need to review **Making a Line Graph.**

Analyze and Conclude

1. **Describe** how the ice in each cup changed.

2. In which cup did the ice change faster?

3. In which cup did the water cool more quickly? What difference between the ice cubes and the crushed ice might explain why the water in one cup cooled faster?

4. Heat energy is needed to melt ice. **Suggest a hypothesis** to explain where the heat energy came from. **Give evidence** to support your hypothesis.

5. The water contained more heat energy at the start of the activity than it did at the end. **Hypothesize** what happened to this heat energy. Support your hypothesis.

INVESTIGATE FURTHER!

EXPERIMENT

Predict the changes that would occur if you added an equal number of ice cubes to both a glass of cold water and a glass of warm water. Try the experiment and check your predictions.

C23

Activity

Speeding Up Change

Wet your finger and hold it up in the air. How does it feel? Does the feeling change when you blow on the finger? What does energy have to do with these changes?

MATERIALS
- dropper
- water
- 4 small dishes
- timer
- *Science Notebook*

Procedure

1. Use a dropper to place a small drop of water in a dish. Place a drop of the same size in a second dish. Set one dish in direct sunlight and the other in a cool, shaded spot. **Predict** what will happen to the two drops of water.

2. Allow the dishes to stand undisturbed, checking on the water drops every few minutes. Each time you check, **record** your observations and the time in your *Science Notebook*.

3. Between observations, **brainstorm** with members of your group. Try to think of ways to make a drop of water evaporate faster. **Record** your suggestions.

4. Put identical drops of water in two dry dishes. Leave one drop alone. **Experiment** with the other drop to see if you can make it evaporate.

5. Repeat step 4 for each technique you try. **Record** each technique and **describe** your results.

Step 4

Analyze and Conclude

1. Which drop of water from step 1 evaporated more quickly? **Suggest a hypothesis** to explain your results.

2. What techniques were successful in causing a drop of water to evaporate faster? Explain why you think each technique was successful.

3. **Make a general statement** about what causes water to evaporate.

C24

Particle Energy

Reading Focus How is the motion of particles involved in changes of state?

Using Math

Water is the only common substance that can be found in all three states of matter at the same time and place. Earth's atmosphere contains only 0.001 percent of all the fresh water on Earth. What fraction is equivalent to 0.001 percent?

Picture in your mind a sample of iron. What do you see? You probably see a hard, grayish solid. This is the state in which iron is usually found. But under the proper conditions, iron can also exist as a liquid. It can even exist as a gas!

Most forms of matter can exist in all three states—solid, liquid, and gas. Perhaps the best example of a substance in all three states is water. You are familiar with water as a solid (ice), a liquid, and a gas (water vapor).

You have also seen water change from one state to another. You have seen ice melt, puddles "dry up," and water vapor change to a liquid and fog up a mirror. In the activities on pages C22 to C24, water

changes from the solid state to the liquid state, and it also changes from the liquid state to the gas state.

Materials change state when energy is added to them or taken away from them. These changes can be understood by thinking about the motion of the particles that make up all matter.

Energy and Temperature

You know from experience that a thrown ball or a falling rock has energy. These objects have energy because of their motion. This energy of motion is called **kinetic energy**. Even the particles that make up matter have kinetic energy because they're moving.

Look back at the drawings on page C21, which show the relative motion of particles in the three states of matter. Would you like to know how fast the particles of a material are moving? Take the material's temperature! **Temperature** is a measure of the average kinetic energy of the particles in a material.

The term *average* indicates that not all particles in a material are moving at the same rate of speed. Some are traveling (or vibrating) a little bit faster or slower than most of the particles.

Temperature and Heat

Many people think that temperature and heat are exactly the same. Although

▲ **Average Versus Total Energy**
The wasps in both of these hives have energy—they are buzzing around. The average speed of the wasps in each hive is the same. But the wasps in the larger hive have more total energy because there are more wasps.

temperature is related to heat, the two are quite different. To help you understand the difference, study the two wasp nests in the drawing.

Now think of a glass of water and a bathtub full of warm water at the same temperature. Just like the wasps, the particles of water in each container have the same average speed. But because there are more particles in the tub, that water would have more heat energy.

Heat energy includes the total kinetic energy of the particles in a material. So a large sample of matter will have more heat energy than a smaller sample of the same matter, even though both samples have the same temperature.

What would happen if you added five or six ice cubes to the warm water in the glass and in the bathtub? The ice cubes in the bathtub would melt more quickly than those in the glass because the water in the tub has more energy to give them.

This example helps to define heat. **Heat** is energy that flows from warmer to cooler regions of matter. In both the glass and the bathtub, energy travels from warm water to cool ice.

Energy and Change of State

Energy is always involved in a change of state. When heat energy is added to a solid at its melting point or a liquid about to evaporate, the temperature does not increase. However, the energy does overcome the forces holding the molecules in solid or liquid form. In the *reverse* processes, energy is released, allowing a liquid or a solid to form.

Water is the best substance to study in order to learn about changes in state. Study the pictures on page C27 as you read about energy and changes of state.

Water Changes State

◄ Ice Changes to a Liquid
The ice absorbs energy from the Sun. This causes the particles to vibrate more. When enough energy has been added, the force holding particles together in the solid is overcome, and the ice changes state, or **melts**, to become liquid water.

◄ Water Changes to a Gas
As more energy is added, particles of liquid water escape and enter the air as a gas. The change of state from liquid to gas is called **evaporation**.

▲ Water as a Gas
Evaporation will continue until all the liquid water has changed into the gas state.

UNIT PROJECT LINK

For this Unit Project you will put on a magic show, using your knowledge of matter. Choose one of the following magic tricks to master.

1. The Disappearing Liquid What happens when you mix two different liquids and some liquid disappears?

2. The Great Tissue Bust How can a tissue be stronger than you are? Find out and then use what you learn in this unit to explain how your trick works.

Technology Link
For more help with your Unit Project, go to **www.eduplace.com**.

Evaporation occurs over a wide range of temperatures and takes place only at the surface of liquid water. If enough heat is added to liquid water, the water will eventually boil. When this happens, bubbles of water vapor form throughout the liquid, as you can see in the picture below. These bubbles will rise through the liquid and escape into the air.

A Change in Direction

Changes in state also take place when heat is removed from water. If enough heat is removed from a gas, it will change to a liquid. This process is called **condensation**. If enough heat is then removed from the liquid, it will change to a solid. This change from a liquid to a solid is called **freezing**. ■

▲ Boiling is rapid evaporation that takes place throughout a liquid at high temperatures.

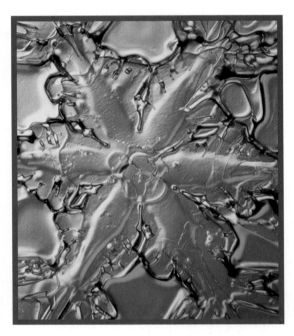

▲ When liquid water freezes, forces between water particles hold them in definite fixed patterns called crystals.

INVESTIGATION 3 WRAP-UP

REVIEW

1. How are temperature and heat different?

2. What happens during condensation?

CRITICAL THINKING

3. Bubbles of gas often form in tap water left at room temperature. Do you think this gas is water vapor, or is it something else? Explain your reasoning.

4. If you put one hand in cold water and the other in hot water, one hand feels cold and the other feels hot. Explain these feelings in terms of the movement of heat.

Word Power

Write the letter of the term that best matches the definition. *Not all terms will be used.*

1. The change of state from a gas to a liquid
2. The amount of mass in a given volume of matter
3. Anything that has mass and volume
4. The amount of space an object takes up
5. Energy that flows from warmer to cooler regions of matter
6. A measure of the amount of matter in an object

a. condensation
b. density
c. evaporation
d. heat
e. mass
f. matter
g. temperature
h. volume

Check What You Know

Write the term in each pair that correctly completes each sentence.

1. To calculate the density of an object, you need to know its volume and its (mass, height).
2. In a liquid the particles move faster than in a (solid, gas).
3. Energy that flows from warmer to cooler regions of matter is known as (heat, temperature).

Problem Solving

1. A 20-mL sample of grayish metal has a mass of 54 g. What is the density of the metal? After you've found its density, use the table of densities on page C14 to identify the metal.

2. Water is an unusual substance in that it expands when it freezes. Use this information to explain why ice cubes float in liquid water.

Study the drawings of the empty box and the football. Then, in your own words, describe how you would determine the volume of each object.

CHAPTER 2

KINDS OF MATTER

Solids, liquids, and gases of countless different kinds make up Earth's lands, waters, and the air. Since prehistoric times, people have used Earth's materials to make things. For example, artists use clay, a kind of matter that comes from the land, to create works of art that are both beautiful and useful.

Connecting to Science
ARTS

Pueblo Pottery Pueblo artist Nancy Youngblood Lugo creates pottery that is known for its bold, fluid designs, which are modern, yet traditional. Youngblood Lugo is a descendant of the Native American Tafoya family, whose name has stood for creativity and excellence in Pueblo pottery through many generations.

The matter in moist clay has the property of being easily shaped. To make one of her pots, Youngblood Lugo first shapes clay into a form. As shown in the photo, she then carves a design on the clay. Another property of clay is its ability to hold its shape after drying and firing. Many artists fire pots in ovens called kilns. But in the traditional way of the Tafoyas, Youngblood Lugo fires her pots in an open flame. At the end of the firing, the flame is put out in a way that changes the matter of the clay to another kind that is hard, shiny, and dark. The finished pots in the lower picture have these properties.

Coming Up

◀ Nancy Youngblood Lugo carving a design on a clay pot called a melon bowl *(top)*, four more clay pieces by the artist *(bottom)*.

How Can Matter Be Classified?

If you were asked to organize all the matter in the world into groups, how many groups do you think you'd need? What characteristics would you choose to identify each group? In this investigation you'll classify matter into two groups: kinds of matter that cannot be broken down and kinds that can.

Activity

Testing Your Metal

Aluminum and copper are kinds of matter. This activity will help you decide which group they belong in.

Procedure

Obtain samples of aluminum and copper. In your *Science Notebook*, list some properties of each of these metals. Brainstorm with members of your group about things you can do to change these samples. Make a list of your ideas and, after getting your teacher's approval, carry out your plans. Describe your actions and record all changes in the samples.

Analyze and Conclude

1. Based on your observations, what properties do copper and aluminum have in common? How are the two metals different?

2. Did any of the changes you caused produce any new materials? Explain your answer.

Activity

A Change for the Wetter

Sugar is a kind of matter. Can sugar be broken down into other materials? Heat some sugar and find out.

- - - - - - - - - - - - - - - - - -

Procedure

1. Sprinkle a small amount of sugar on a sheet of black paper. Examine the grains of sugar with a hand lens. Make a sketch of a sugar grain in your *Science Notebook*.

2. Obtain about a half spoonful of sugar. Place a candle in the center of a shallow dish and ask your teacher to light the candle. Using a potholder, hold the spoon over the candle so that the flame just touches the bowl of the spoon.

3. While you heat the sugar, have your partner use tongs to hold a glass square 2–3 centimeters above the sugar.

4. Observe the sugar and the glass square carefully. Continue heating the sugar until all the white crystals have disappeared. Record your observations of the sugar and the glass.

MATERIALS

- goggles
- sugar
- black construction paper
- hand lens
- metal spoon
- candle
- shallow dish
- potholder
- tongs
- glass square
- *Science Notebook*

SAFETY

Wear goggles. Be very careful when working around open flames. Secure loose clothing and tie back long hair. Avoid touching melted candle wax and heated sugar. They can cause painful burns.

Analyze and Conclude

1. What was the first sign that a change was taking place?

2. Compare the appearance of the material in the spoon at the end of the activity with the sugar you started with. What evidence is there that you've produced different kinds of matter from the sugar?

3. What appeared on the glass square? Infer where this material came from.

Step 2

Elements

Reading Focus What are elements, and how are they organized?

Look at the familiar materials in the photographs on this page. These materials are all different, yet they have at least one thing in common—they are all kinds of matter.

Matter can be identified by its properties, or characteristics. **Physical properties** are characteristics that can be measured or detected by the senses. Color, size, odor, and density are examples of physical properties. **Chemical properties** describe how matter changes when it reacts with other matter. The fact that paper burns is a chemical property of paper.

Given time, you could probably list hundreds or even thousands of kinds of matter. Yet scientists are able to classify all matter into two large groups—substances and mixtures. These two groups can be divided into smaller groups, as shown in the graphic organizer on page C35.

A **substance** is a material that always has the same makeup and properties, wherever it may be found. Of the materials shown in the photographs below, gold, aluminum, sugar, and water are all substances. Milk is a mixture. A **mixture** is a combination of two or more substances. You will learn about mixtures later in this chapter.

There are two kinds of substances—elements and compounds. An **element** is a substance that cannot be broken down by simple means into any other substance. The activity on page C32 shows that aluminum and copper cannot be changed into simpler kinds of matter. Aluminum and copper are elements.

A **compound** is a substance made up of two or more elements that are chemically combined. Water and sugar are examples of compounds. In the activity on page C33, sugar is changed

What properties can be used to identify these different materials? ▼

milk

water

gold

aluminum

sugar

Classifying Matter

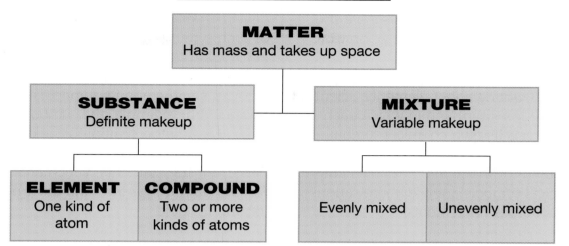

MATTER
Has mass and takes up space

SUBSTANCE
Definite makeup

MIXTURE
Variable makeup

ELEMENT
One kind of atom

COMPOUND
Two or more kinds of atoms

Evenly mixed

Unevenly mixed

into simpler substances. One is water. The black material remaining in the spoon is an element, carbon.

Identifying Elements

Elements have been described as the building blocks of matter. All matter, regardless of its form, is made up of one or more elements. What, then, are elements made of?

Recall that all matter is made up of very tiny particles. Think about cutting a small piece of aluminum in half and then cutting one of the halves in half. Now imagine continuing to divide the aluminum into smaller and smaller pieces. Eventually you would have a particle so small that it could not be divided anymore and still be aluminum.

The tiny particle would be a building block of aluminum—an aluminum atom. An **atom** is the smallest particle of an element that has the chemical properties of the element.

All the atoms that make up a particular element are the same. Gold, for example, is made up only of gold atoms. Aluminum atoms make up the element aluminum. Gold atoms differ from aluminum atoms,

and both gold atoms and aluminum atoms differ from the atoms of all other elements.

Today scientists know of 112 elements. Each element is made up of only one kind of atom. This means that there are 112 different kinds of atoms.

Ninety elements are found in nature. These elements include many familiar substances, such as iron, copper, iodine, aluminum, and tin. But many unfamiliar elements exist too, such as ruthenium (rσσ thē′nē əm), francium (fran′sē əm), and xenon (zē′nän). From just these 90 elements are built the many kinds of matter that make up the whole universe!

Technology Link
CD-ROM

INVESTIGATE FURTHER!

Use the **Science Processor CD-ROM**, *Nature of Matter* (Investigation 2, Sorting Space Stuff) to explore a new planet and test the materials you discover. Decide which ones are compounds, which ones are mixtures, and which ones are elements.

Twenty-two of the known elements are not found in nature. These elements are known only because scientists have produced them artificially in the laboratory.

Chemical Symbols

When writing about elements, scientists use a kind of shorthand in which each element has its own chemical symbol. A **chemical symbol** is one or two letters that stand for the name of an element. Chemical symbols are like abbreviations for the names of elements.

For many elements, the symbols come from the elements' names in English or other modern languages. Some examples of such symbols include O for oxygen, H for hydrogen, and Ca for calcium.

Sometimes the connection between an element's name and its symbol is not so obvious. For example, the symbol for iron is Fe and the symbol for gold is Au. These symbols come from the Latin names for the elements, which are *ferrum* (fer′əm) for iron and *aurum* (ô′rəm) for gold.

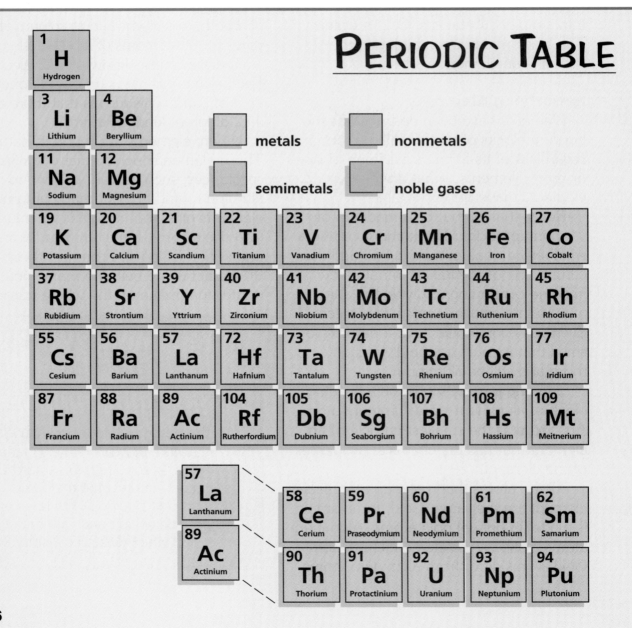

PERIODIC TABLE

metals   nonmetals
semimetals   noble gases

| 1 H Hydrogen |
| 3 Li Lithium | 4 Be Beryllium |
| 11 Na Sodium | 12 Mg Magnesium |

19 K Potassium	20 Ca Calcium	21 Sc Scandium	22 Ti Titanium	23 V Vanadium	24 Cr Chromium	25 Mn Manganese	26 Fe Iron	27 Co Cobalt
37 Rb Rubidium	38 Sr Strontium	39 Y Yttrium	40 Zr Zirconium	41 Nb Niobium	42 Mo Molybdenum	43 Tc Technetium	44 Ru Ruthenium	45 Rh Rhodium
55 Cs Cesium	56 Ba Barium	57 La Lanthanum	72 Hf Hafnium	73 Ta Tantalum	74 W Tungsten	75 Re Rhenium	76 Os Osmium	77 Ir Iridium
87 Fr Francium	88 Ra Radium	89 Ac Actinium	104 Rf Rutherfordium	105 Db Dubnium	106 Sg Seaborgium	107 Bh Bohrium	108 Hs Hassium	109 Mt Meitnerium

| 57 La Lanthanum |
| 89 Ac Actinium |

| 58 Ce Cerium | 59 Pr Praseodymium | 60 Nd Neodymium | 61 Pm Promethium | 62 Sm Samarium |
| 90 Th Thorium | 91 Pa Protactinium | 92 U Uranium | 93 Np Neptunium | 94 Pu Plutonium |

The Periodic Table

The idea that there are certain basic kinds of matter—elements—is an old one. Some early scientists thought there were four elements—fire, earth, air, and water. However, by the seventeenth century, scientists had identified a number of elements. By the nineteenth century, more than 50 elements were known.

In 1869 a Russian chemist, Dmitri Mendeleev, published a table of the 63 elements known at that time. Mendeleev organized the elements into a table according to the weights of their atoms and their properties. The elements in each column of the table had similar properties. The table below is a modern version of Mendeleev's table. It is called the Periodic Table of Elements.

Each block of this periodic table includes information about a particular element. For example, hydrogen is the simplest element. That is, hydrogen atoms have the simplest structure. For this reason, hydrogen is listed first and it is given the atomic number 1.

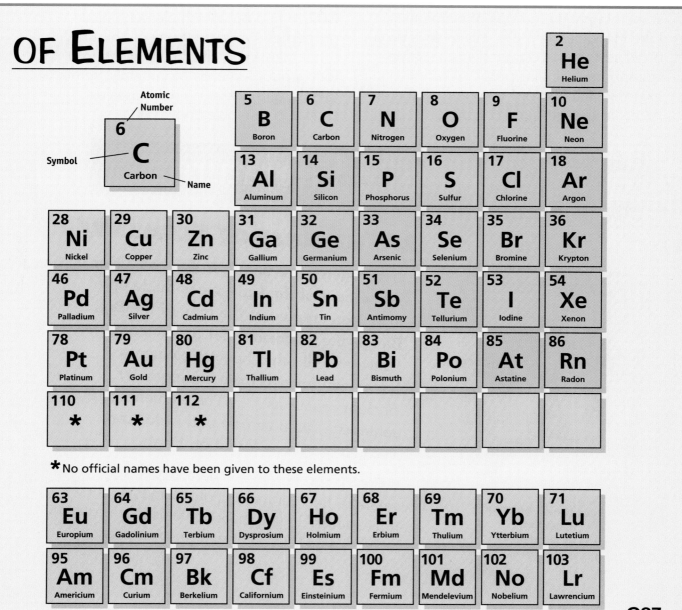

OF ELEMENTS

* No official names have been given to these elements.

Classifying Elements		
Group	Examples	Properties
Metals	iron, copper, aluminum	Usually shiny; can be formed into sheets and wire; good conductors of heat and electricity
Nonmetals	sulfur, carbon, chlorine	Dull; cannot be easily shaped; poor conductors of heat and electricity; some are gases
Semimetals	silicon, boron	Have some properties of both metals and nonmetals
Noble Gases	helium, neon, radon	Do not combine readily with other elements

Using the Periodic Table

In addition to information about each element, the periodic table tells you something about groups of elements. Like Mendeleev's table, this table is organized so that the elements in the same column have similar properties. For example, except for hydrogen, all the elements in the left-hand column are chemically active metals. All the elements in the right-hand column are inactive gases. Use the table on pages C36 and C37 to find out which elements have properties similar to those of chlorine.

Elements can also be classified into four groups—metals, nonmetals, semimetals, and noble (nō'bəl) gases as shown in the table above. ■

Science in Literature

A UNIVERSE OF ELEMENTS

Eyewitness Science: Chemistry
by Dr. Ann Newmark
Dorling Kindersley, 1993

"Hydrogen is the simplest element. Over 90 percent of the Universe is made up of hydrogen created at the time of the Big Bang—the explosion that produced the Universe. All other heavier elements have been formed from hydrogen by nuclear reactions. . . . The elements in a meteorite, such as iron and nickel, are identical to those found on Earth. . . ."

Read *Eyewitness Science: Chemistry* by Dr. Ann Newmark to find out more about elements. For example, which do you think contains more oxygen, air or Earth's crust? The answer may surprise you.

Compounds

Reading Focus How are compounds formed?

One of the most beautiful materials found in the laboratory is a reddish-orange powder sometimes known as red precipitate (prē sip'ə tit). The photographs show what happens to this powder if you heat a small amount of it in a test tube.

In the photographs you can see the contents of the test tube change from a reddish-orange solid to a dark powder and then to a shiny liquid on the sides of the test tube. What you can't see is the gas escaping from the mouth of the test tube. How can you tell that red precipitate is *not* an element?

The Composition of Compounds

Red precipitate is a compound of mercury and oxygen. Its scientific name is mercuric (mər kyoor'ik) oxide, and it

forms when the elements mercury and oxygen combine. When elements combine to form a compound, their atoms become chemically linked, or joined. In most compounds, such as water, the linked atoms form **molecules** (mäl'i kyo͞olz). In some compounds, such as salt, or sodium chloride, the atoms are held together in hundreds or thousands of units, forming crystal-like structures.

When elements join to form compounds, the joined elements lose their original properties and take on new ones. For example, mercury is a shiny liquid metal. Oxygen is a colorless, invisible gas. But as you have seen, the compound made up of these elements, mercuric oxide, is a reddish-orange powdery solid.

▼ **As it is heated, mercuric oxide separates into mercury and oxygen.**

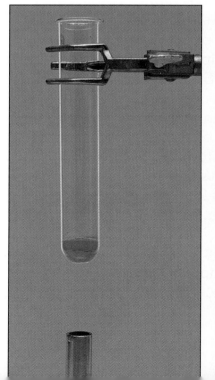
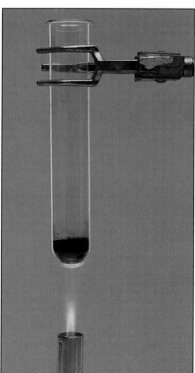
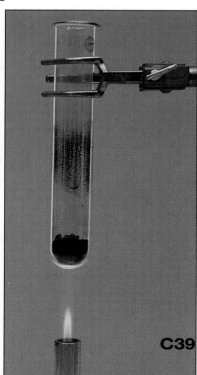

▲ Sodium is a soft metal that reacts explosively with water.

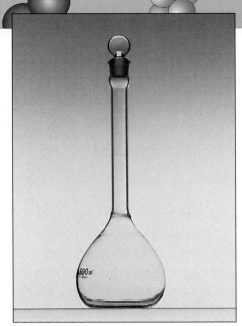

▲ Chlorine is a poisonous, greenish-yellow gas.

Water and salt are two common substances that show how much elements can change when they combine to form compounds. Water is a compound made up of the elements hydrogen and oxygen, which are both colorless gases. Hydrogen burns with a very hot blue flame. Oxygen helps other substances to burn but does not burn itself.

So what are the properties of the compound that is made when these two gases combine with each other? Water is a liquid that does not burn. In fact, it can be used to put out fires!

Sodium chloride (commonly known as table salt) is made up of sodium and chlorine. The photographs above show what these elements are like. It's hard to believe that the white crystals you sprinkle on your popcorn are made up of such dangerous elements!

Chemical Formulas

Just as chemical symbols are used to represent elements, chemical formulas are used to represent compounds. A **chemical formula** is a group of symbols that shows the elements in a compound. For example, the chemical formula for water is H_2O. This formula shows that a single molecule of water is made up of 2 hydrogen atoms and 1 oxygen atom.

In the formula for water, look at the number 2 after the symbol for hydrogen. A number written to the right of and below a symbol in a chemical formula is called a subscript (sub'skript). A subscript shows how many atoms of an element are present in a single molecule or the simplest unit of a compound.

No subscript is written to show a single atom. So if you don't see a subscript in a formula (as with the O in H_2O), you can assume that there is one atom of that element. The formula for sulfuric acid, for example, is H_2SO_4. This formula shows that each unit of sulfuric acid contains 2 atoms of hydrogen, 1 atom of sulfur, and 4 atoms of oxygen.

Compounds of Carbon

Many compounds found in nature are very complex. This is especially true of compounds of carbon. Carbon is an element that is found in all living things. An entire field of chemistry, called organic chemistry, is devoted to the study of carbon compounds.

The table sugar you put on your cereal in the morning has the chemical formula $C_{12}H_{22}O_{11}$. How many atoms make up a single molecule of this compound? Does this sound like a giant, complex molecule? Not when it's compared with a particle of cholesterol (kə les'tər ôl).

Cholesterol is a compound found in the cells of many living things. Although cholesterol plays some important roles in living organisms, an excess of the compound can cause serious health problems, such as heart disease, in humans. The chemical formula for cholesterol is $C_{27}H_{45}OH$.

How many atoms are present in a single molecule of cholesterol? You would probably agree that this molecule is, indeed, complex. But carbon is a very "linkable" atom. The number of different carbon compounds is seemingly endless. And many of these compounds are more complex than cholesterol. ■

Eggs and fried foods are sources ▶ of cholesterol.

UNIT PROJECT LINK

Here are some more magic tricks. Choose one to work on with your group.

1. What Color Is Blue Ink? Is ink a mixture or a compound?

2. The Invisible Force Can an index card be used as a cap to keep a glass full of water from spilling?

3. The Leakproof Strainer How can one liquid keep another liquid from passing through the holes in a strainer?

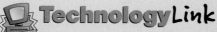

Technology Link

For more help with your Unit Project, go to **www.eduplace.com**.

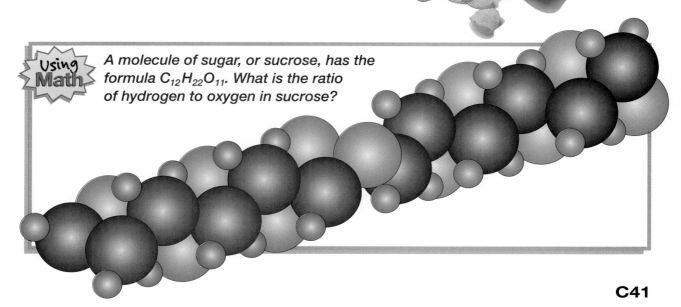

Using Math

A molecule of sugar, or sucrose, has the formula $C_{12}H_{22}O_{11}$. What is the ratio of hydrogen to oxygen in sucrose?

Ancient Elements

Reading Focus How has our understanding of elements changed over time?

Chemistry got its start as an experimental science in the Middle Ages with the alchemists (al'kə mists). The goal of the alchemists was not scientific knowledge. Alchemists were mainly interested in wealth and long life. Much effort was spent trying to change iron and lead into gold and searching for a substance that could give everlasting life.

Though many of the ideas of the alchemists were wrong, much good came from their efforts. At least five elements and many chemicals were discovered or identified by alchemists. The time line shows that alchemists helped pave the way for modern chemistry. ■

The term *element* is coined by Plato, a famous Greek philosopher. The Greeks consider the four basic kinds of matter, or elements, to be fire, water, air, and earth.

400–300 B.C.

The earliest metal objects are made. In the Middle East, small jewels and tools are carved or cut from gold, copper, and silver.

10,000 B.C.

1550 B.C. Plows made of bronze are used in what is now Vietnam.

3200 B.C.
Copper is mined on a large scale in Egypt. Copper is used in the making of bronze during the Bronze Age.

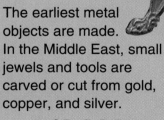

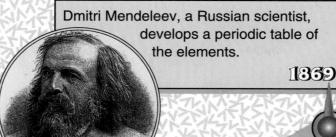

Dmitri Mendeleev, a Russian scientist, develops a periodic table of the elements.

1869

1803

English chemist John Dalton proposes his atomic theory.

1661

English chemist Robert Boyle re-introduces the idea of basic types of matter called elements.

A.D. 700–1300

Science declines in Europe and thrives in the Arab world. Chemistry develops into an experimental science through the efforts of the alchemists. They learn many things about how elements behave and combine with each other.

INVESTIGATION 1 WRAP-UP

REVIEW

1. What do elements and compounds have in common? How do they differ?

2. What is the meaning of the formula H_2O?

CRITICAL THINKING

3. The formula for carbon dioxide is CO_2. The formula for sulfur trioxide is SO_3. The formula for carbon tetrachloride is CCl_4. Infer the meanings of the prefixes *di-*, *tri-*, and *tetra-*.

4. A certain element has the atomic number of 53. What is its name and symbol? Is it more similar to oxygen or to chlorine? Explain.

INVESTIGATION 2

WHAT IS A MIXTURE?

Perhaps the two most common kinds of matter at Earth's surface are rocks and ocean water. Neither is a substance. Both kinds of matter are made up of different elements and compounds mixed together. Find out about mixtures in this investigation.

Activity

Working With Mixtures

How can you tell if something is a mixture? With some things, such as chocolate chip ice cream or vegetable soup, it's easy to tell. With others, such as vanilla ice cream or salt water, it's more difficult.

Procedure

1. Cut a piece of aluminum foil and a piece of copper foil into small pieces. Add the pieces to a clear jar.

2. Add 2 or 3 spoonfuls of sugar to the jar. **Predict** whether the properties of any of the materials in the jar will be changed by being mixed together. Place the lid on the jar and shake the jar vigorously.

MATERIALS
- goggles
- scissors
- aluminum foil
- copper foil
- sugar
- 2 clear jars with lids
- spoon
- hand lens
- aquarium gravel
- sand
- *Science Notebook*

SAFETY

Wear goggles. Be careful working with scissors.

Step 2

3. Use a hand lens to examine the contents of the jar carefully. In your *Science Notebook*, **describe** the contents of the jar and tell how you would separate the parts of this mixture.

4. Add 2 spoonfuls each of aquarium gravel and sand to another jar. Cover the jar and shake it vigorously.

5. Brainstorm with your partner to **plan an experiment** for separating the parts of the sand-gravel mixture. After showing the plan to your teacher, obtain the necessary materials and carry out your plan.

6. Return the sand and gravel to the jar. Add 2 spoonfuls of sugar to the jar and repeat step 5 for this mixture.

Step 3

Analyze and Conclude

1. Were any properties of the aluminum, copper, or sugar changed by being mixed together? How do you know?

2. What can you **infer** about the differences between a mixture and an element? a mixture and a compound?

3. **Describe** your method for separating the mixture of sand and gravel. Were you able to use the same method to separate the mixture of sand, gravel, and sugar? Why or why not? If not, **describe** the method you used to separate this mixture.

Step 4

INVESTIGATE FURTHER!

EXPERIMENT

Wearing disposable gloves and goggles, mix a spoonful of sand and a spoonful of iron filings. Think of a property of iron that you could use to help separate this mixture. Write up a plan for separating the mixture. Show the plan to your teacher. If the plan is approved, carry it out.

Activity
Racing Colors

Is black ink a substance or a mixture? Find out if you can separate it into parts.

MATERIALS

- water
- wide-mouth jar
- scissors
- filter paper
- water-based black ink marker
- rubber band
- *Science Notebook*

SAFETY

Handle scissors with care.

Procedure

1. Fill a jar with water to within a few millimeters of its rim.

2. Cut a small hole in the center of a piece of filter paper. Use a water-based black ink marker to make a circle of round dots near the hole in the filter paper, as shown.

3. Stretch the filter paper over the mouth of the jar and hold it in place with a rubber band.

4. Cut a second piece of filter paper in fourths. Roll up one of the fourths to make a cone. Insert the tip of the cone through the hole in the filter paper covering the jar until it touches the water.

5. **Predict** what will happen as water moves up the cone and past the marker spots. **Record** your prediction in your *Science Notebook*.

6. **Observe** the setup until the water has reached the edge of the jar. **Record** your observations.

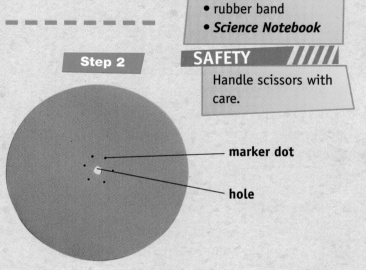

Step 2

marker dot

hole

Step 4

Analyze and Conclude

1. **Describe** what happens to each marker spot.

2. Is ink a substance or a mixture? What evidence can you give to support your answer?

Activity

A Mixed-Up State

Some mixtures behave like a liquid. Some behave like a solid. The behavior of some mixtures, as you will discover, is not easy to describe.

Procedure

1. Place four or five spoonfuls of cornstarch in a dish. **Predict** how the cornstarch will change if you add water to it.

2. Add several drops of food coloring to some water in a plastic cup. Add this colored water, a few drops at a time, to the cornstarch. Stir with a tongue depressor until you have a wet ball of cornstarch.

3. Describe the material you have created. Pick some up and **observe** its properties. **Record** your observations in your *Science Notebook*.

4. Try cutting the material with a plastic knife. Try rolling it into various shapes. Place marbles on the material and describe what happens.

Step 2

Analyze and Conclude

1. Why is the material produced in this activity a mixture?

2. **Describe** the ways that the material acts like a liquid and the ways it acts like a solid.

3. Do you think the mixture can easily be separated into its original parts? Explain your answer.

Mixtures

Reading Focus How is a mixture different from a compound?

The chemical formula for water is H_2O. This formula tells you that water is made up of 2 parts hydrogen and 1 part oxygen. Is water a mixture of hydrogen and oxygen? This question may confuse people who are just beginning to study chemistry. The answer to the question is no. About the only thing that compounds and mixtures have in common is that each is made up of two or more different kinds of matter.

Keeping Their Properties

In the activity on pages C44 and C45, aluminum, copper, and sugar are mixed together in a jar. Even after shaking the jar, it is still possible to recognize the different substances that make up the mixture.

This activity provides a clue as to how mixtures are different from compounds. All the substances in a mixture keep their original properties. When substances combine to form a compound, the properties of the substances that make up the compound are gone. The properties of these substances are replaced by the unique properties of the compound.

Suppose you were to mix iron filings with salt. No matter how thoroughly you mixed the two substances, you would still have iron and salt. Both substances would still have their original properties. For example, one physical property of iron is that it is attracted to a magnet. Mixing the iron with salt has no effect on this property, as the photograph below shows.

◀ Iron is magnetic, and it keeps this property in a salt-iron mixture.

▲ **Is this fruit punch a mixture or a compound?**

When substances combine to form a compound, the substances change. Water, for example, is nothing like the hydrogen and oxygen that combine to make up water. And water's properties are very different from those of hydrogen and oxygen.

The Makeup of a Mixture

Ice cream is a mixture—perhaps one of your favorite mixtures. There are many varieties, or flavors, of ice cream, and each contains different ingredients.

Mixtures, including the various flavors of ice cream, don't have chemical formulas. The reason is that two mixtures of the same materials can be quite different in makeup. This explains why the same flavor of ice cream may taste different from brand to brand.

To understand how mixtures of the same materials can differ, think about two bowls of fruit punch made with the same ingredients. One person might mix two bottles of orange juice, one bottle of club soda, some strawberries, some cherries, and a cut-up orange. Using the same ingredients, someone else might mix one bottle of orange juice, two bottles of club soda, and the same kinds of fruit but in different amounts.

Both would have mixtures of liquids and fruit, but the mixtures would not be the same throughout. So a single formula could not accurately represent the make-up of such a mixture.

Unlike a mixture, a compound *always* has the same composition. For example, no matter where it comes from, salt always contains one part sodium and one part chlorine. Water always contains two parts hydrogen and one part oxygen. That's why you can use a chemical formula to represent a compound. The chemical makeup of a given compound never changes.

Some Common Mixtures

Most matter in the world around you exists as mixtures. You just have to look out the window to see evidence of this. In fact, the glass in your classroom windows is a mixture. Most window glass is made up of silicon dioxide (sil'i kän dī äks'īd) and some other substances. Most glass is pretty much the same, but the amount of each substance in glass can vary from sample to sample without affecting the properties of the glass.

Beyond your classroom window you can probably see a variety of materials, such as bricks, cement, and asphalt (as'fôlt). All these building materials are mixtures. As you observe these mixtures, you are looking through, and are surrounded by, a very important natural mixture—air.

Air is a mixture of gases. This mixture consists of about four-fifths nitrogen gas and one-fifth oxygen gas. But air also contains small amounts of other gases, such as carbon dioxide and water vapor. The percentages of these gases vary from place to place and from time to time.

You don't have to look outside the classroom to find mixtures. In fact, you don't have to look any further than your own body. The human body contains many different mixtures. Blood, sweat, tears, and saliva are a few examples of mixtures that make you what you are.

Separating Mixtures

The different materials in a mixture can almost always be separated from each other by some physical means. For example, a variety of methods are used to

▲ The composition of air changes from time to time and place to place.

separate different mixtures in the activity on pages C44 and C45.

The method used to separate a mixture depends on some difference in the physical properties of the materials in the mixture. One important property used in separating a mixture is the size of the pieces making up the mixture. Suppose, for example, you had a pocketful of coins—pennies, nickels, dimes, and quarters. You could easily separate this mixture by hand.

Now suppose you get a job in a store. At the end of the week, you are asked to separate a shopping bag full of coins. You could do this by hand, but it would take quite a while. A sorting machine like the one shown would make the job of separating the coins easier.

A mixture of salt and sand would be more difficult to separate than a mixture of coins. It would be almost impossible to separate the materials by hand. And a sorting machine wouldn't work, because the pieces of salt and sand are similar in size. So you have to find another method for separating the mixture.

Think about salt and sand. Do either of these materials have some property you could use to separate them? Yes, salt dissolves in water and sand does not. If you

▲ **What properties of coins does this machine use to separate a mixture of coins?**

What property or properties could you use to separate a mixture of coins? ▶

add water to a mixture of salt and sand, the salt will dissolve in the water. You can then pour off the salt water and collect the sand, which remains behind. How might you get the salt back from the salt water? ■

───────── **INVESTIGATION 2 WRAP-UP** ─────────

REVIEW

1. Explain why a mixture cannot be represented by a chemical formula.

2. What is the difference between a mixture and a substance?

CRITICAL THINKING

3. Suppose you had a mixture of iron pellets, pebbles, and small wood spheres, all about the same size. How would you separate this mixture?

4. How can mixtures of the same substances differ?

C51

INVESTIGATION 3

WHAT ARE LIQUID MIXTURES LIKE?

What do milk, soft drinks, and ocean water have in common? Your first thought may be that they are all liquids. But if you consider it more carefully, you'll realize that they are all liquid mixtures. Study the properties of these mixtures in this investigation.

Activity

Mixing Solids Into Liquids

Sugar dissolves in water and seems to disappear. What factors affect how fast the sugar disappears?

MATERIALS
- goggles
- 3 plastic cups
- water
- marker
- sugar cubes
- stirring rod
- timer
- spoon
- *Science Notebook*

Procedure

1. In your *Science Notebook*, **make a chart** like the one shown.

Conditions	Time
Cold Water	
Water at Room Temperature	
Warm Water	
Warm Water + Stirring	
Warm Water + Crushed Sugar + Stirring	

See **SCIENCE** and **MATH TOOLBOX** page H11 if you need to review **Making a Chart to Organize Data.**

2. Fill one cup with ice-cold water, a second cup with water at room temperature, and a third cup with warm water. Use equal amounts of water in each cup. Use a marker to label the cups as shown here.

3. **Predict** which water will most quickly dissolve a sugar cube. Then add a sugar cube to each cup. Time how long it takes for each sugar cube to dissolve. **Record** the times in your chart.

4. Pour out the water and rinse the cups. Refill one cup with warm water and add a sugar cube. This time, stir the mixture until the sugar cube dissolves. **Record** the time.

5. Use a spoon to crush a sugar cube. Repeat step 4, using the crushed sugar. **Record** the time.

Step 4

Analyze and Conclude

1. How did the temperature of the water affect the rate at which the sugar dissolved in it?

2. What effect did stirring have on the rate at which the sugar dissolved in water?

3. What effect did crushing the sugar into small particles have on the rate at which the sugar dissolved?

4. What can you **infer** about the size of the sugar particles that are dissolved in a mixture of sugar and water?

5. **Suggest a hypothesis** that relates the effects of water temperature, stirring, and smaller pieces of sugar to the rate at which sugar dissolves.

INVESTIGATE FURTHER!

EXPERIMENT

Once salt is dissolved in water, how can you get the salt back? Design an experiment to get the salt out of salt water.

Activity

To Mix or Not to Mix

Shake that bottle of salad dressing before you pour it on your salad. If you don't, you may get only part of the mixture.

Procedure

1. Add water to a jar until it is about one-fourth full.

Math Hint *To estimate the one-fourth line of a container, measure the height of the container and round the height to the nearest whole unit. Then divide by 4.*

2. Add a few drops of food coloring to the water. Swirl the water around in the jar until the water is evenly colored throughout.

3. Add the same amount of vegetable oil to the jar as you did water. Screw the lid tightly on the jar.

4. Shake the jar several times and stand it on the table. **Observe** what happens to the liquids in the jar. **Record** your observations in your *Science Notebook*.

5. Turn the jar upside down and hold it that way. **Observe** what happens to the liquids and **record** your observations.

Step 3

Step 4

Analyze and Conclude

1. Does water mix with food coloring? **Give evidence** to support your answer.

2. Do water and oil mix? **Give evidence** to support your answer.

3. What happened when you turned the jar upside down?

4. Based on your observations, what can you **infer** about the ability of different liquids to mix?

Activity

Making Water Wetter

What happens if you try to clean a greasy dish with plain water? The water runs off the dish. The water doesn't seem to wet the dish. Can you mix something with water to make it "wetter"?

Procedure

1. Spread a sheet of wax paper on the table.

2. Use a dropper to carefully place one drop of an unidentified blue liquid on the paper. Use a toothpick to probe the drop and observe how it behaves. In your *Science Notebook*, record your observations, including the color of the drop and what shape the drop takes.

3. Using a clean dropper, place a drop of an unidentified red liquid on the paper. Use the toothpick to probe the drop and observe how it behaves. Record your observations.

4. Repeat step 3 with a drop of plain water.

Step 3

Analyze and Conclude

1. Describe the shapes of the two colored drops and compare their behavior when you probed them with a toothpick.

2. One colored liquid is plain water mixed with food coloring; the other is water mixed with food coloring and detergent. Infer which is which. Give evidence to support your inference.

3. Which liquid seemed to "wet" the wax paper better?

4. Suggest a hypothesis to explain how detergent in water helps clean grease.

What's the Solution?

Reading Focus What factors affect the rate at which solutions form?

When viewed from space, Earth is a lovely planet. Satellite photographs of our planet show cloud patterns, oceans, and continents—in other words, air, sea, and land. These three nonliving parts of our planet are mixtures. Air is a mixture of many gases. Rocks are mixtures of minerals. And sea water is a mixture of water and different minerals, mainly salts.

More Mixing

Look back at the graphic organizer on page C35. Notice that mixtures are divided into two groups—unevenly mixed and evenly mixed. Most mixtures fall into the unevenly mixed group.

Suppose you added equal amounts of sand, salt, and sugar to a container. You could try everything to mix the materials evenly, but some parts of the mixture would be just a little different from the other parts. For example, one part of the mixture would contain a few more grains of salt or sand or sugar than another part of the mixture.

Now think of a sugar-water mixture. The sugar and the water mix so completely that the solid sugar seems to disappear. If you could take samples from different parts of the mixture, you would find that every part is exactly the same as every other part.

When sugar mixes with water, the sugar spreads evenly throughout the water and seems to disappear. ▼

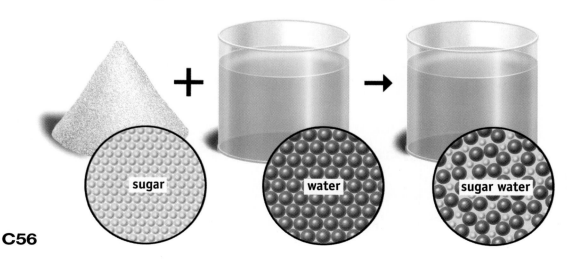

sugar   water   sugar water

◀ Salad dressing is an example of a suspension. A suspension is a liquid mixture in which some particles are temporarily suspended in the mixture.

Even after it is shaken, the salad ▶ dressing is not a solution. If the bottle is left to stand, the dressing separates into its different parts.

Solutions Are Not Puzzling

A mixture in which the different particles of matter are spread evenly throughout is called a **solution**. A solution has two main parts. The **solvent** (säl'vənt) is the material that is present in the greater amount. The **solute** (säl'yo͞ot) is the material present in the smaller amount.

You are probably most familiar with solutions formed when a solid solute, such as sugar, dissolves in a liquid solvent, such as water. You might be surprised to learn that there are other types of solutions. For example, bronze is a solution of two metals, tin and copper.

Rate of Solution

Which dissolves faster in water—a sugar cube or a spoonful of loose sugar grains? Dissolving takes place only on the surface of the sugar, where the water is in contact with the sugar. Small cubes, or grains, of sugar dissolve faster than a large sugar cube. The drawing below shows why.

Temperature also affects the rate at which things dissolve. For example, sugar dissolves faster in hot water than in cold water. The particles of hot water are moving faster and have more energy than the particles of cold water. The fast-moving particles bump into the sugar harder and more frequently, helping to break the sugar into smaller pieces.

Stirring a mixture also helps speed up the rate at which things dissolve. Stirring causes the particles of solute to mix more quickly with the particles of solvent. ■

Internet Field Trip

Visit **www.eduplace.com** to find out more about solutions.

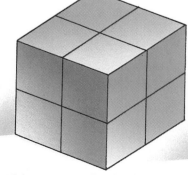

▲ This sugar cube has six sides. Each side has a surface area of 4 cm². The total surface area of this cube is 6 × 4 cm² = 24 cm².

◀ This is the same amount of sugar. The total surface area of 1 small cube is 6 × 1 cm². There are 8 small cubes. So the total surface area of 8 cubes is 8 × 6 cm² = 48 cm².

Bubbles

Reading Focus How can the force of attraction between water molecules be changed?

HOW IT Works

Have you ever seen a water strider? A water strider is an insect that is able to walk on water! How does the water strider manage to stay on the water's surface? If you look very closely at the surface, it seems to be covered with a very thin skin. The shape of the water strider's feet allow the insect to glide across this skin without breaking it.

A force of attraction called cohesion exists among water particles. This force produces an effect called surface tension, which is responsible for the "skin" on the water's surface.

Have you ever tried to produce large bubbles like the one shown, using plain water? It's not possible. In fact, because of cohesion, you can't even get water to form a film on the bubble wand. But if you add a little soap to the water, it's a different story. Like the girl in the picture below, you can form delicate bubbles that float in the air.

When soap is added to water, it reduces the forces of attraction among water particles. Surface tension is also greatly reduced. If the water strider stepped onto the surface of soapy water, the insect would enjoy a swim rather than a stroll.

▲ Reduced cohesion makes it possible for the soap-water mixture to be stretched out into a thin film, or bubble. Some soap bubbles are no more than one or two particles in thickness.

Alloys

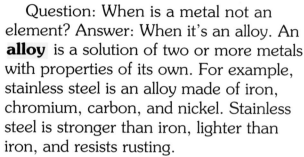

Question: When is a metal not an element? Answer: When it's an alloy. An **alloy** is a solution of two or more metals with properties of its own. For example, stainless steel is an alloy made of iron, chromium, carbon, and nickel. Stainless steel is stronger than iron, lighter than iron, and resists rusting.

An alloy is made by melting two or more metals and mixing them together. The mixture is then allowed to cool and harden to a solid. In its final form an alloy consists of a solution in which the metal components are thoroughly mixed with each other.

Some Important Alloys

Alloys have been important to humans for thousands of years. One of the first alloys ever prepared was bronze, which is a mixture of copper and tin. Some bronzes also contain zinc.

The earliest bronze items have been dated at about 3500 B.C. The introduction of bronze was such an important event that a whole period in human history—the Bronze Age—has been named after this alloy.

▲ **These bronze objects are more than 1,000 years old.**

Common Alloys

Alloy	Composition	Use
Brass	70% Cu, 30% Zn	hardware, plumbing
Bronze	90% Cu, 10% Sn	artwork, domes of buildings
Gold alloy	70% Au, 15% Ag, 10% Cu, 1% Pt, 1% Zn, 1% Pd	dentistry, jewelry
Pewter	85% Sn, 7% Cu, 6% Bi, 2% Sb	cups, candlesticks
Solder	60% Pb, 40% Sn	connecting metal pieces together
Stainless steel	74% Fe, 18% Cr, 8% Ni	cutlery
Steel	99% Fe, 1% C	bridges, buildings
Sterling silver	93% Ag, 7% Cu	jewelry, tableware

The table above lists some common alloys and tells what metals they contain and how they are used. Refer to the periodic table on pages C36 and C37 for the names of the metals whose chemical symbols are given.

Alloys are useful because their properties are different from those of the metals from which they are made. For example, alloys of gold are much harder and less expensive than pure gold. A unit called a karat (kar′ət) is used to express the purity of a sample of gold.

Amalgams (ə mal′gəmz) are alloys that contain mercury. An amalgam used in dental work consists of 70 percent silver, 18 percent tin, 10 percent copper, and 2 percent mercury. The mercury makes the amalgam soft enough for a dentist to work with it.

Some alloys have unusual properties. For example, Wood's metal is an alloy of bismuth (biz′məth), lead, tin, and cadmium (kad′mē əm). This alloy has a melting point of 70°C. It will melt on your stove at a relatively low temperature setting. Can you see how this alloy can be used in automatic sprinklers?

Another interesting alloy is misch (mish) metal, which is made of cerium (sir′ē əm), lanthanum (lan′thə nəm), and other metals. Misch metal has the unusual property of giving off sparks when it is rubbed. Because of this property, misch metal is used in the manufacture of flints used for lighting butane stoves. ■

INVESTIGATION 3 WRAP-UP

REVIEW

1. Explain why salad dressing is not a solution.

2. What do compounds and mixtures have in common?

CRITICAL THINKING

3. Why is an alloy both a mixture and a solution?

4. What methods would you use to dissolve a large crystal of salt, known as rock salt, in water? Explain all the factors that affect the rate at which the salt will dissolve.

REFLECT & EVALUATE

CHAPTER 2 REVIEW

Word Power

Write the letter of the term that best matches the definition. *Not all terms will be used*.

1. Characteristics that can be measured or detected by the senses

2. The smallest particle of an element that has its chemical properties

3. A group of symbols that show the elements in a compound

4. Characteristics that describe how matter changes when it reacts with other matter

5. A group of atoms that are chemically linked

6. A solution of two or more metals

a. alloy
b. atom
c. chemical formula
d. chemical properties
e. element
f. molecule
g. physical properties
h. solvent

Check What You Know

Write the term in each pair that correctly completes each sentence.

1. Metals, nonmetals, semimetals, and noble gases are four different types of (elements, compounds).

2. When elements are joined in a compound, they (lose, keep) their original properties.

3. Glass is a (mixture, compound).

4. When soap is added to water, its surface tension (increases, decreases).

Problem Solving

1. Explain why all the elements that appear in the same column of the periodic table are commonly referred to as a family.

2. How could you quickly separate a mixture of brass tacks and iron tacks?

3. Explain why salt cannot be removed from a salt-water mixture by pouring the mixture through a paper filter.

Study the section of the periodic table shown. Use the section to determine which elements are more similar in chemical and physical properties—copper and zinc, or copper and silver. Explain how you know.

| 29 Cu Copper | 30 Zn Zinc |
| 47 Ag Silver | 48 Cd Cadmium |

CHAPTER 3

HOW MATTER CHANGES

Have you ever been camping? A good campfire may have helped warm you. A campfire builder usually has to cut large pieces of wood into smaller pieces for the fire. When this wood burns, it leaves only ashes. In this chapter you'll find out about the physical and chemical changes that matter undergoes.

PEOPLE USING SCIENCE

Bioprospector Petrona Rios collects plants and insects in the rain forests of Costa Rica. As a bioprospector (bī ō prä'spek-tər), she gathers these specimens so that chemists can analyze them for their potential use in developing new medicines.

Along with other bioprospectors, Petrona Rios continually crisscrosses the rain forest, gathering plant and insect specimens. The collected specimens are processed at INBio (Instituto Nacional de Biodiversidad) and sent to the University of Costa Rica. There, chemists make samples of the materials and send them to a major drug company. Chemists at the drug company thoroughly test the samples, looking for substances that can be used in new medicines.

As the samples are tested, they go through many chemical and physical changes. What chemical and physical changes do you see every day?

C62

Coming Up

◀ Petrona Rios (*center*) with student assistants

INVESTIGATION 1

HOW CAN MATTER CHANGE?

You can tear a piece of paper into hundreds of smaller pieces. Yet each piece, no matter how small, is still paper. You could recycle the small pieces and make new paper from them. But what would you have if you were to burn the paper? Find out about changes that matter can undergo in this investigation.

Activity

Balloon Blower

Blowing up a balloon can be a lot of work. How would you like to have a balloon that inflates by itself? In this activity you can combine some materials and make an automatic balloon inflater with the changes that result.

MATERIALS
- goggles
- balloon
- funnel
- measuring spoon
- baking soda
- vinegar
- narrow-necked bottle
- *Science Notebook*

SAFETY
Wear goggles during this activity.

Procedure

1. Blow up a balloon and let the air out several times. This action will stretch the rubber, making the balloon easier to inflate.

2. Place the stem of a funnel in the neck of the deflated balloon. Pour two spoonfuls of baking soda into the balloon. Gently shake the balloon to make sure the baking soda settles to the bottom of the balloon. Remove the funnel from the balloon.

3. Add several spoonfuls of vinegar to a narrow-necked bottle.

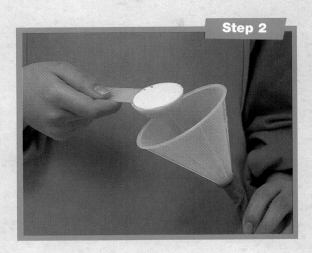
Step 2

4. Stretch the opening of the balloon over the mouth of the bottle, as shown in the picture. Make sure no baking soda escapes from the balloon.

5. Lift the balloon and hold it above the bottle so that the baking soda falls into the bottle.

Step 4

6. Observe the changes that take place when the baking soda mixes with the vinegar. Record your observations in your *Science Notebook*.

Analyze and Conclude

1. A **chemical change** involves the formation of new substances. What evidence is there that a chemical change took place inside the bottle after the baking soda dropped into the vinegar?

2. What happened to the balloon? From your observation, what can you infer about one of the substances produced when vinegar and baking soda react?

3. Hypothesize about the action of the baking soda and vinegar. Are both substances still present, or have they changed into new types of matter? Give evidence to support your hypothesis.

Technology Link CD-ROM

INVESTIGATE FURTHER!

Use the **Science Processor CD-ROM**, *The Nature of Matter* (Investigation 3, More Matter?) to travel back in time to 1789 and visit Antoine Lavoisier's laboratory. Conduct an experiment to find out what happens when you heat tin.

Activity

Making a Fire Extinguisher

In the last activity a chemical change produced a gas. In this activity you can see why this gas makes a useful fire extinguisher.

Procedure

1. Add three spoonfuls of vinegar to one jar and one spoonful of baking soda to another jar.

2. Place a candle in the center of a shallow dish and ask your teacher to light the candle. Ignite a fireplace match by holding it at the end and placing the tip of the match in the candle flame.

3. Insert the burning match first into the jar containing baking soda and then into the jar containing vinegar, as shown in the picture. Do not allow the flame to touch the contents of the jars. Look for any changes in the flame and then blow out the match. Record your observations in your *Science Notebook*.

4. Hold the jar containing baking soda firmly on the tabletop while you carefully pour the vinegar into this jar. Describe what happens.

5. Light another fireplace match by holding it in the candle flame and then blow out the candle. Insert the tip of the burning match into the jar containing the vinegar and baking soda. Observe what happens and record your observations.

Analyze and Conclude

1. Oxygen must be present for burning to take place. Infer whether oxygen was present above the baking soda and the vinegar in each jar before you mixed these materials. Explain what your inference is based on.

2. What inferences can you make about the gas released when you mixed the vinegar and the baking soda? Give evidence to support your inferences.

Step 3

Activity

Solids From Liquids

If you have ever made water turn into ice, you've made a solid from a liquid. In this activity you'll make a solid from two liquids by causing a chemical change.

Procedure

1. Obtain samples of unknown liquids *A* and *B*. Study the liquids and **record** your observations in your *Science Notebook*.

2. Mix the two liquids by carefully pouring the contents of one container into the other container.

Step 2

3. **Observe** the mixture for five minutes. **Record** any changes you observe.

Analyze and Conclude

1. What did you observe happening when you mixed the two liquids together?

2. What evidence indicates that the change you observed taking place was a chemical change?

3. **Hypothesize** whether liquids *A* and *B* are the same material or different materials. Support your hypothesis.

Physical and Chemical Change

Reading Focus How are chemical changes different from physical changes?

Picture yourself in this situation. You're getting ready to go to a party. You're all dressed except for your favorite wool sweater, which just came from the cleaners. You take the sweater from its protective plastic and pull it on. But it's too small—much too small!

You take the sweater off and hold it up. It's about half the size it's supposed to be! At first you think the cleaners gave you the wrong sweater. But the name tag sewn inside tells you it's your sweater. What went wrong?

Changing but Staying the Same

The case of the shrunken sweater is an example of a physical change. A **physical change** is a change in the size, shape, or state of a material. No new matter is formed during a physical change. The wool of the sweater is still the same. It just takes up less space now!

You see physical changes every day. When you sharpen a pencil or rub chalk on the board, you cause physical changes to take place. The pencil shavings and the chalk dust produced by your actions are different from the objects they came from. But the shavings are still made up of wood, and the dust is still made up of chalk.

In nature, physical changes can turn one kind of landscape into another. For example, over many millions of years, a river can carve its way down through solid rock to form a deep canyon. Pounding waves, over time, can transform rock cliffs into fine sand. In both cases, the rocks may be changed in size and appearance, but they are still made of the same substances.

Water is a good substance to use when studying physical changes. Many substances dissolve in water. The act of dissolving is a physical change. Changes in state—melting, freezing, evaporation, and condensation—are physical changes.

Why is making a baseball bat from a piece of wood an example of a physical change? ▼

Changing but *Not* Staying the Same

Have you ever smelled milk that has turned sour? Do you think that sour milk is the same as fresh milk? Whole milk is a mixture. When bacteria from the air digest part of the mixture, changes occur and a new substance, called lactic acid, is produced. This change is similar to the one that occurs when two liquids are mixed together in the activity on page C67. Any change in which one or more new substances are formed is a **chemical change**.

Water can also be changed chemically. Recall that water is a compound made up of the elements hydrogen and oxygen. The drawing shows how water can be changed into its component elements.

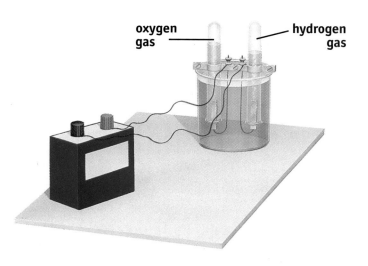

oxygen gas ——— ——— hydrogen gas

▲ **An electric current can be used to separate water into oxygen gas and hydrogen gas. The gases can be collected in test tubes.**

Chemical changes are common in nature. The rusting of iron is one example of such a change. Rust is produced when oxygen from the air combines with iron. The product is neither iron nor oxygen, but a new substance called iron oxide, or rust.

▲ **Plants use energy from sunlight to change water and carbon dioxide gas into sugar. Plants use the sugar as food.**

▲ **Animals use plants as food. Chemical changes occur when food is digested. These chemical changes release energy that animals need to grow and be active.**

▲ **Some chemical changes are not helpful. For example, rusted parts on a bicycle don't move smoothly and may even crumble.**

Describing Chemical Changes

Chemical changes are triggered by chemical reactions. In a chemical reaction, one or more substances interact to form new substances. When describing what happens during a chemical reaction, scientists often use symbols and formulas to write "chemical sentences." These sentences are written in the form of equations, much like those used in math problems.

Suppose you wanted to describe the reaction in which water is broken down into hydrogen and oxygen. The chemical equation for this reaction is shown here.

$$2H_2O \longrightarrow 2H_2 + O_2$$

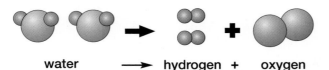

water $\longrightarrow$ hydrogen + oxygen

If you wanted to express this reaction in words, you would say that two molecules of water break down to produce two molecules of hydrogen gas and one molecule of oxygen gas. In this equation, the arrow is read as *produce*, and the plus sign is read as *and*.

Look at the equation for the reaction in which iron and oxygen combine to produce iron oxide, or rust.

$$4Fe + 3O_2 \longrightarrow 2Fe_2O_3$$

How would you write this chemical sentence in words?

Many changes, such as the freezing of water to form ice, are physical. No new substances are formed. Other changes, such as those that occur when a fuel is burned or a piece of iron rusts, result in new substances being formed. Such changes are chemical changes. ■

Science in Literature

HOW METALS REACT

"Potassium and tin behave differently when put into contact with water. Potassium . . . reacts vigorously, and so much heat is generated that the hydrogen gas produced catches fire and burns with a lilac flame. Tin . . . reacts hardly at all with water. If diluted acid is used, potassium reacts even more vigorously, and tin reacts very slowly to produce hydrogen."

Look at page 25 of *Eyewitness Science: Chemistry* by Dr. Ann Newmark, to see pictures of these reactions. Then read on to find out about many other chemical changes.

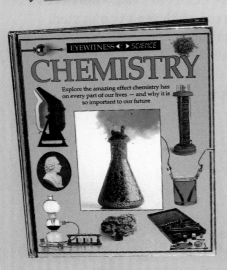

Eyewitness Science: Chemistry
by Dr. Ann Newmark
Dorling Kindersley, 1993

Atomic Structure and Chemical Change

> **Reading Focus** What are the parts of an atom, and how are they arranged in a Bohr model?

Imagine that the marbles in the picture are elements. Suppose you were asked to arrange the marbles to make as many different substances as possible. You are told that a substance can have as few as one element and as many as five. How many different substances can you make in two minutes?

Now think about the 112 known elements. How many different substances can be made from these elements? Now you have some idea about how it is possible to have so many different kinds of matter on Earth.

What Is a Model?

All chemical changes involve atoms. So if you want to understand what's happening when a match burns, when iron rusts, or when milk sours, you need to know more about atoms.

Atoms, of course, are much too small to be seen, even with the most powerful microscope. How then do scientists learn about atoms? Just about everything known about atoms has been learned from indirect evidence. This evidence is gathered by studying how matter behaves in all kinds of chemical reactions.

Based on this evidence, scientists have developed various models of the atom. In science, a **model** is a way to represent an object or to describe how a process takes place. Models are often used to describe things that are too big or too small to be studied directly. For example, a globe is a model of Earth.

What Is an Atom Like?

Modern scientific models of the atom describe it as being made up of several different tiny parts. These tiny parts are called protons (prō′tänz), neutrons (noo′tränz), and electrons (ē lek′tränz).

Most of the mass of an atom is contained in a dense, central core called a **nucleus** (noo′klē əs). This nucleus contains protons and neutrons. A **proton** is a particle with a positive electric charge. A **neutron** is a particle with no electric charge.

Traveling around the nucleus, at some distance from it, are one or more electrons. An **electron** is a particle with a negative electric charge.

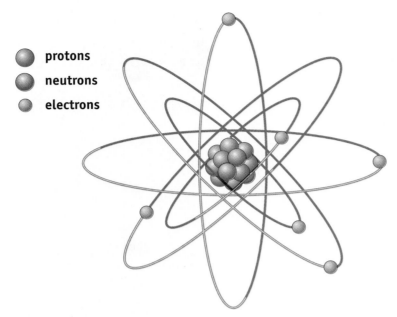

- ● protons
- ● neutrons
- ● electrons

◀ The drawing shows a model of a carbon atom. This atom has six protons and six neutrons in its nucleus and six electrons outside the nucleus. This type of atomic model is known as a Bohr model, after Niels Bohr, the Danish physicist who developed it.

Two Models—Old and New

Look at the Bohr models of a helium atom and a lithium (lith′ē əm) atom below. Notice how the electrons are shown moving around the nucleus in paths called orbits. The helium atom has one orbit and the lithium atom has two orbits. A Bohr model is also called a planetary model of the atom. Why do you think this is so?

Bohr suggested his model in 1913. As scientists learned more about atoms, they found that electrons do not travel in definite orbits. Rather, they "swarm" around the nucleus, much like bees swarm around a hive.

Because electrons travel so fast, they can be thought of as a "cloud" surrounding the nucleus. The drawing below shows an electron cloud model of a helium atom.

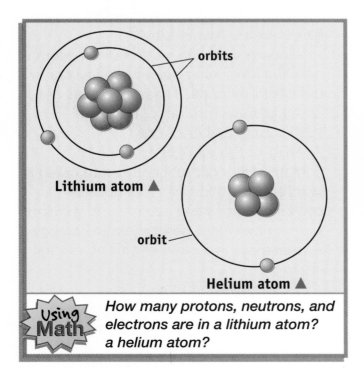

orbits

Lithium atom ▲

orbit

Helium atom ▲

Using Math

How many protons, neutrons, and electrons are in a lithium atom? a helium atom?

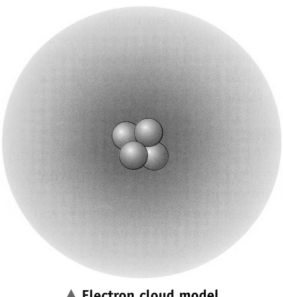

▲ **Electron cloud model of a helium atom**

Roles of Protons and Electrons

The number of protons in the nucleus of an atom gives the atom its identity. An atom of hydrogen has one proton. An atom of oxygen has eight protons. That's what makes hydrogen what it is and oxygen what it is.

Recall from the periodic table on pages C36 and C37 that *every element has a different atomic number.* The **atomic number** of an element is the number of protons in an atom of that element. The atomic number of hydrogen is 1. Look at oxygen in the periodic table. What is the atomic number of oxygen?

Electrons are the smallest and lightest of the three types of atomic particles. Yet, because electrons move around outside the nucleus, they determine how an atom reacts with other atoms. In other words, the electrons that surround the nucleus of an atom give the atom its chemical properties.

Atoms With a Charge

Usually the number of protons in an atom equals the number of electrons. So the positive and negative charges balance each other. This balance leaves the atom electrically neutral.

Sometimes, however, an atom may capture one or more electrons from another atom. When this happens, both atoms become electrically charged. An electrically charged atom is called an **ion** (ī'ən). The drawing shows how positive and negative ions are formed.

Because they have opposite charges, positive and negative ions attract each other. If the attraction is strong enough, the ions are held tightly together and form an ionic compound, such as sodium chloride. Ionic compounds are not made up of molecules. Instead, the basic unit of any ionic compound is made up of one or more positive ions and one or more negative ions.

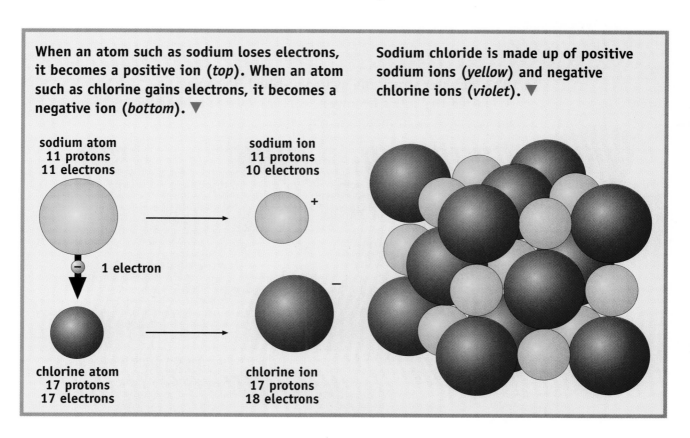

When an atom such as sodium loses electrons, it becomes a positive ion (*top*). When an atom such as chlorine gains electrons, it becomes a negative ion (*bottom*). ▼

sodium atom
11 protons
11 electrons

sodium ion
11 protons
10 electrons

+

1 electron

−

chlorine atom
17 protons
17 electrons

chlorine ion
17 protons
18 electrons

Sodium chloride is made up of positive sodium ions (*yellow*) and negative chlorine ions (*violet*). ▼

Atoms and Molecules

Many compounds, such as water, are made up of molecules. In forming molecules, atoms don't gain or lose electrons. Instead they share electrons. For example, when hydrogen reacts with oxygen to form water, two hydrogen atoms and one oxygen atom join up by sharing electrons, as shown in the drawing.

It is as if the oxygen atom is holding hands with two hydrogen atoms. Think of each hand as an electron. And think of each pair of clasped hands as a chemical bond between the atoms. Chemists call this type of compound a covalent compound.

Making and Breaking Bonds

Energy is always involved in the making or breaking of chemical bonds. Usually when bonds form between atoms, energy is given off. However, sometimes a little energy must be added to get such a reaction started. For example, a little spark is needed to get hydrogen to combine with oxygen. But once the reaction starts,

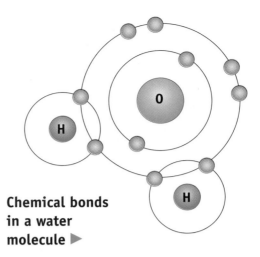

Chemical bonds in a water molecule ▶

energy is given off rapidly, as shown in the photograph below.

Energy is also involved in breaking chemical bonds. Recall the description on page C69 of how water can be broken down into hydrogen and oxygen by passing electricity through it. The electricity provides the energy needed to break the bonds between the hydrogen atoms and oxygen atoms that make up water. ■

Internet Field Trip

Visit **www.eduplace.com** to find out more about chemical bonding.

In 1937, disaster struck the hydrogen-filled *Hindenburg*. A spark ignited the ship's hydrogen, and energy was released as the hydrogen combined with oxygen in the air. ▼

Conservation of Mass

Reading Focus What is the law of conservation of mass?

When a piece of wood burns, the mass of the ashes that remain is less than the mass of the original piece of wood. On the other hand, when a piece of tin is heated, it gains mass. Three hundred years ago, these and similar observations led scientists to wonder: Is matter destroyed when wood burns? Is matter created when tin is heated?

Over the years the work of many scientists provided answers to these and other questions about matter. For example, when wood burns, some of its mass goes into gases that are produced. These gases escape into the air. Today we know that matter cannot be created or destroyed by any chemical reaction. This statement of fact is known as the law of conservation of mass.

Albert Einstein publishes his theory of relativity, which includes the equation $E = mc^2$. This theory establishes the relationship between mass and energy.

1905

Working independently, two scientists—Karl Wilhelm Scheele and Joseph Priestley—discover oxygen.

A.D. 1772–1774

1890–1910
Marie Curie's work with radium leads to a better understanding of radioactivity.

450 B.C.
Greek philosophers Leucippus (lōō sip′əs) and Democritus (di mäk′rə təs) first state the ideas set forth in the law of conservation of mass.

1789
Antoine Lavoisier, a French chemist, discovers that when matter such as tin burns, it combines with oxygen. This discovery leads to the law of conservation of mass.

Radioactive Elements

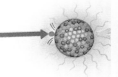

On March 1, 1896, French scientist Henri Becquerel wrapped a sheet of photographic film in paper that light couldn't penetrate. He placed the package in a desk drawer, together with a few small rocks, and closed the drawer.

A few days later, Becquerel developed the film, expecting to see an unexposed white negative. Instead he was shocked to see darkened areas on the film. Something had changed the chemicals on the film—but what?

▲ Becquerel discovers radioactivity.

Nuclear Radiation

Becquerel's film had been exposed to nuclear radiation (rā dē ā'shən), invisible energy that came from the rocks. The rocks contained the radioactive element uranium (yoo rā'nē əm). A **radioactive element** is made up of atoms whose nuclei (*nuclei* is the plural of *nucleus*)

break down, or decay, into nuclei of other atoms. When a radioactive element decays, it changes into a different element. This happens because some of the radiation released by the decaying nucleus is in the form of protons and neutrons. And when an atom loses protons from its nucleus, its atomic number changes.

Recall that an element is identified by its atomic number. The drawing shows how a uranium nucleus decays to form a thorium (thôr'ē əm) nucleus. Notice how the atomic number changes from 92 to 90.

When a nucleus decays, large amounts of energy are released. The particles released from the nucleus will have lots of energy. Sometimes high-energy rays called gamma rays are produced as well.

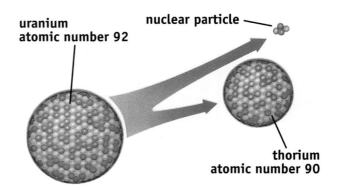

uranium atomic number 92

nuclear particle

thorium atomic number 90

▲ When a uranium nucleus decays, it loses 2 protons and 2 neutrons, leaving a nucleus with 90 protons. The element with atomic number 90 is thorium.

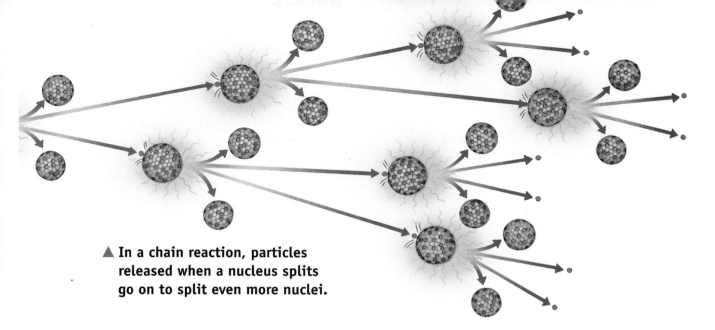

▲ In a chain reaction, particles released when a nucleus splits go on to split even more nuclei.

Using Energy From Atoms

Radioactive elements occur naturally. Scientists have also learned how to split the nuclei of some atoms by bombarding them with neutrons. This reaction is called **nuclear fission** (nōo′klē ər fish′ən). *Fission* means "splitting."

The drawing above shows how neutrons are used to split nuclei of uranium atoms. Two new atoms are produced each time a nucleus splits. Also, some single neutrons and energy are released. Some of these neutrons collide with and split other nuclei, producing a chain reaction.

An uncontrolled nuclear chain reaction releases energy so fast that an explosion takes place. A nuclear reactor is a device in which a nuclear chain reaction is controlled. In a controlled chain reaction, energy is released slowly.

Radiation—Helpful and Harmful

Nuclear reactors provide energy that is used to generate electricity. Reactors are also used to make radioactive forms of many elements. These elements are used in medical research and in the treatment of certain illnesses.

Clearly, nuclear energy has many uses that are beneficial. But nuclear radiation can also damage human tissues. Thus, radioactive materials must be handled safely and must not be allowed to get into the environment by accident. ■

INVESTIGATION 1 WRAP-UP

REVIEW

1. How does heating sugar in a spoon differ from dissolving it in a cup of hot water?

2. Write the following chemical equation in words.

$$2H_2O \longrightarrow 2H_2 + O_2$$

CRITICAL THINKING

3. When might a Bohr model of an atom be more helpful than an electron cloud model?

4. If two neutrons escaped the nucleus of an atom, what would be the effect on the atom's atomic number and its total electric charge?

WHAT ARE ACIDS AND BASES?

Vinegar, orange juice, soap, baking soda, and antacid tablets are all things you can probably find around your home. Some of these materials are acids, and some are bases. In this investigation you'll find out what acids and bases are and how to use some simple tests to tell the difference.

Activity

Cabbage-Juice Science

Some substances, called indicators, are one color in an acid and a different color in a base. In this activity you can see for yourself how an indicator works.

- -

Procedure

1. In your *Science Notebook,* make a chart like the one shown.

Cup	Material	Observation
1	Vinegar	
2	Lemon juice	
3	Baking soda	
4	Powdered lime	

See **SCIENCE and MATH TOOLBOX** page H11 if you need to review *Making a Chart to Organize Data.*

MATERIALS

- goggles
- 6 small plastic cups
- juice of a red cabbage
- marker
- 2 droppers
- vinegar
- lemon juice
- baking soda
- powdered lime (calcium oxide)
- pineapple juice
- liquid soap
- *Science Notebook*

SAFETY

Wear goggles during this activity. Do not touch or taste any chemicals.

Step 3

2. Half fill four small plastic cups with red cabbage juice and number the cups with a marker.

3. Use a dropper to add a few drops of vinegar to the cabbage juice in cup 1. Use a clean dropper to add a few drops of lemon juice to cup 2. **Record** in your chart any changes that you observe.

4. Add a small amount of baking soda to cup 3 and a small amount of powdered lime to cup 4. **Record** any changes that you observe.

5. **Predict** what would happen if you tested red cabbage juice with pineapple juice and with liquid soap. Carry out the tests in clean cups and check your predictions.

6. **Predict** what would happen if you added vinegar to the cup containing the baking soda and cabbage juice. Carry out the test. **Record** your results.

Step 4

Analyze and Conclude

1. In which cups did chemical changes occur? How do you know?

2. Cabbage juice is an indicator. What evidence is there that some of the materials you tested are acids or bases?

3. **Infer** which of the materials is the most similar to vinegar. **Give evidence** to support your inference. These materials are acids.

4. **Classify** all the substances you tested into two groups, based on how they react with the cabbage-juice indicator.

INVESTIGATE FURTHER!

EXPERIMENT

Use additional cabbage juice to test different liquids, including plain water and carbonated water. Group the liquids by the color changes they produce.

Activity
The Litmus Test

Litmus paper is an indicator. Blue litmus paper turns red in an acid. Red litmus paper turns blue in a base. See if you can identify the acids and bases in this activity.

Procedure

1. In your *Science Notebook*, make a chart like the one shown.

Solution	Red Litmus Paper	Blue Litmus Paper
A		
B		
C		

2. Place a piece of red litmus (lit'məs) paper and a piece of blue litmus paper beside three containers labeled *A*, *B*, and *C*. Remember, blue litmus paper turns red in an acid; red litmus paper turns blue in a base.

3. Dip the tip of a piece of blue litmus paper and the tip of a piece of red litmus paper in each liquid. Leave each piece of litmus paper beside the container in which it was dipped.

4. Observe each piece of litmus paper for any change in color. In your chart, record your observations.

Step 2

Analyze and Conclude

1. Which liquids were acids? How do you know?

2. Which liquids were bases? How do you know?

3. Write a rule for using litmus paper to identify a liquid that is neither an acid nor a base.

Step 3

Acids, Bases, and Salts

Reading Focus How can you find out if a compound is an acid or a base?

It's a brutally hot day, and you've just finished mowing the lawn. Now you're looking forward to a cool, refreshing drink of lemonade. You take the pitcher from the refrigerator, pour yourself an ice-cold glass, and take a deep gulp. Immediately your mouth puckers and your eyes begin to water. It's not lemonade—it's lemon juice! And is it sour!

Although you didn't mean to, you have just discovered a telltale property of some important chemical compounds—acids. And you used a test that you wouldn't be able to use in the laboratory—the taste test.

Telltale Colors

Compounds have certain properties that can be used to classify them. Acids and bases are two important groups of compounds. As the pictures below show, these compounds are found in many household products.

One property of acids and bases is the effect they have on indicators (in'di kāt-ərz). An **indicator** is a substance that changes color when mixed with an acid or a base. Cabbage juice is used as an indicator in the activity on pages C78 and C79. In the activity on page C80, paper treated with an indicator called litmus is used to test for acids and bases.

ACIDS The substances below are acids. An **acid** is a compound that turns blue litmus paper red. ▼

BASES The substances below are bases. A **base** is a compound that turns red litmus paper blue. ▼

As the pictures on page C81 show, the effects of acids and bases on litmus can be used to define these compounds.

Some Properties of Acids and Bases

As you would learn if you drank some lemon juice, acids have a sour taste. Some acids, like the natural acids in foods, are weak. Vinegar and citrus fruits are foods that contain acids. Boric (bôr'ik) acid is safe enough to be used in eyewash solutions.

Strong acids, such as sulfuric (sul-fyŏŏr'ik) acid, are dangerous—they are poisonous and can burn the skin. Many acids, even some weak ones, are *corrosive*—they eat away metals and other substances. Digestive juices produced by your stomach contain a strong acid.

However, the acid is very dilute (di lŏŏt'). This means that small amounts of the acid are mixed with large amounts of water. Diluting strong acids helps to reduce their harmful effects.

Bases taste bitter and feel slippery. Like acids, some bases are weak and some are strong. Examples of weak bases include baking soda, which is used in cooking, and antacid tablets, which are used for upset stomachs.

Strong bases, like strong acids, are poisonous and can burn the skin. Sodium hydroxide (hī dräks'īd), commonly known as lye, is an example of a strong base. Sodium hydroxide is used in soap making and in drain cleaners.

The pH Scale

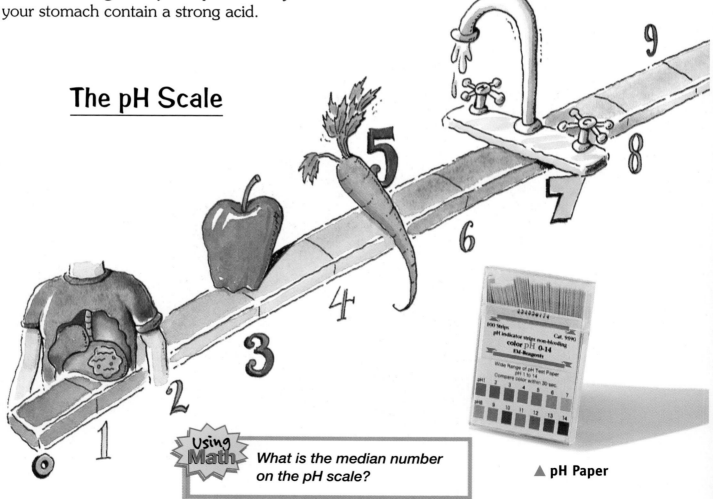

Using Math What is the median number on the pH scale?

▲ pH Paper

The Strong and the Weak

Acids and bases are usually found dissolved in water. For example, lemon juice and orange juice are solutions of citric acid in water. If you add a small amount of acid to a large volume of water, the solution won't be very acidic. On the other hand, if you add a large amount of acid to a small volume of water, the solution might be very acidic.

There's a way to measure how acidic or how basic a solution is. The acidic or basic strength of a solution is measured on a scale known as the pH scale.

The pH scale has units from 0 to 14. The smaller the unit, the more acidic a solution is. The larger the unit, the more basic it is. So a solution with a pH of 1 or less would be very acidic. On the other hand, a solution with a pH near 14 would be very basic. Solutions with a pH near the middle of the scale are neutral. Pure water has a pH of 7.

How can you find the pH of a solution? Indicator paper made with special dyes is used for this purpose. The paper turns different colors depending upon how acidic or basic the solution is that's being tested.

Canceling Out Each Other

Have you ever heard someone complain of having acid indigestion, or heartburn? This condition occurs when the stomach produces too much acid, resulting in a burning sensation.

Antacid tablets, which are weak bases, are often used to relieve this condition. The word part *ant* in the term *antacid* comes from the prefix *anti-*, which means "against" or "opposed to." The base in the tablet reacts with the acid and cancels out, or neutralizes (nōō′trə līz əz), its effects.

The reaction between an acid and a base is called **neutralization** (nōō trə li-zā′shən). When an acid and a base react, two substances—water and a salt—are produced. A **salt** is a compound that can be formed when an acid reacts with a base. The properties of water and salt are very different from those of the acids and bases that react to produce them. ■

UNIT PROJECT LINK

Work to perfect one of these tricks for your magic show.

Crystal Creation Make crystals appear in a liquid.

Great Burnout Make a flame go out as if by magic.

Parting Pepper Make pepper grains scatter across the surface of a liquid without disturbing the liquid.

Dissolving Pictures Use a magic solution to transfer a picture from a newspaper onto a piece of paper.

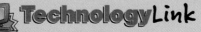 TechnologyLink
For more help with your Unit Project, go to **www.eduplace.com**.

Acid Rain

A gentle wind blows constantly across the land. As the wind travels, it sweeps across cities, villages, factories, and power plants like an invisible broom. And like a real broom, the wind carries all sorts of dirt along with it. This dirt includes soot, dust, and smoke. It also includes a number of harmful gases.

Pickup and Delivery

When the wind moves over farm areas, it picks up dust and may pick up traces of fertilizers or chemicals used to control weeds and insects. Over cities and industrial regions, the wind picks up gases produced by the burning of gasoline, coal, and oil. These gases include compounds of sulfur and of nitrogen.

Where acid rain is "born" ▼

Acids From the Sky

As sulfur and nitrogen compounds mix with water in the air, they react to produce two strong acids—sulfuric acid and nitric acid. At first these acids are dissolved in tiny droplets of water that remain in the air. They are part of the clouds that form and drift across the sky. However, over time these droplets begin to collect into larger and larger drops. Eventually the drops are too heavy to stay in the air, and they begin to fall as rain, snow, sleet, or hail.

If you were to measure the pH of this precipitation, also known as acid rain, you might discover readings as low as 2.0. Acid solutions that are this strong can do serious damage to both living and nonliving things. People in many parts of

Modern windmills use clean wind energy to generate electricity. ▶

the world have suffered from lung, skin, and eye irritations related to acid rain .

The stone and metal of famous statues and well-known buildings have been damaged or eaten away by acids from the sky. Forests and lakes in many regions of the world have been severely affected by acid rain. In Germany's Black Forest, acid rain has killed trees covering an area of more than 5,000 km² (2,000 mi²). In Sweden, thousands of lakes have become so acidic that most plants and many species of fish can no longer live in them. Similar events and conditions have been reported in many areas of the world, including the United States and Canada.

What can be done to stop the destruction caused by acid precipitation? The obvious answer is to reduce air pollution. The major source of air pollution is the burning of fossil fuels—coal, oil, and gas. These are the fuels we use to run our cars, heat our homes, produce our electricity, and power our factories.

Scientists and engineers worldwide are seeking ways to reduce dependency on fossil fuels. Some promising alternative sources of energy are being used. These sources include hydroelectric plants, which use the energy of moving water to generate electricity. Other sources of clean energy being explored are wind energy and solar energy.

In cases where fossil fuels are commonly used—such as in power plants, factories, and automobiles—methods have been developed to keep pollutants from escaping into the air. Various measures for reducing air pollution are being used in many countries. After all, sulfuric acid—or its acidic relatives—belongs in a container, not in a cloud. ■

INVESTIGATION 2 WRAP-UP

REVIEW

1. How are acids and bases alike? different?

2. When would you use an indicator?

CRITICAL THINKING

3. A solution has a pH of 11. What effect would such a solution have on litmus paper? How would you neutralize this solution?

4. What are some ways you and your family can help prevent acid rain?

WHAT DO CHEMISTS DO?

Suppose you read about a mysterious material beneath the Antarctic icecap that scientists have discovered. How would you learn about such a material? A chemist would study its chemical and physical properties. You can do the same thing.

Activity
Mystery Powders

Imagine that you find six jars, each containing a different powder. On the floor near the jars, you find six labels—sugar, salt, baking soda, cornstarch, powdered milk, and plaster of Paris. How will you identify the powders?

Procedure

1. Study the table on page C87. It contains information about the appearance and behavior of six materials.

2. In your *Science Notebook*, **make a chart** with the same headings as the table on the next page, but don't fill in your chart yet. Instead of names of substances in column 1, **record** the letters *A* through *F*.

3. Sprinkle a sample of one powder on a sheet of black construction paper. **Observe** the powder with a hand lens. Under the heading *Appearance*, In the appropriate row, **record** how the powder looks. Repeat this step for each mystery powder.

MATERIALS
- goggles
- mystery powders in jars labeled *A* through *F*
- black construction paper
- hand lens
- aluminum foil
- 3 droppers
- water
- toothpicks
- plastic spoons
- vinegar
- solution of iodine
- *Science Notebook*

SAFETY
Wear goggles during this activity. Do not touch or taste any of the chemicals in this activity.

Name	Appearance	Water	Vinegar	Iodine
Sugar	white; grains of different shapes	dissolves, forming clear solution	no reaction	no reaction
Salt	white; small crystal cubes	dissolves, forming clear solution	no reaction	no reaction
Baking soda	small grains of different shapes	dissolves, forming clear solution	bubbles form	no reaction
Cornstarch	white powder; tiny particles	forms gooey mixture	no reaction	turns dark blue
Powdered milk	white powder; tiny particles	forms cloudy mixture	no reaction	no reaction
Plaster of Paris	white powder; tiny particles	forms cloudy mixture that slowly hardens	no reaction	no reaction

4. Place three small samples of one mystery powder on a piece of foil. Add a few drops of water to one sample and stir the mixture with a toothpick. **Record** your observations. Add vinegar to the second sample and iodine to the third. Mix and **observe** each sample and **record** your observations.

5. Repeat step 4 for each mystery powder.

Step 4

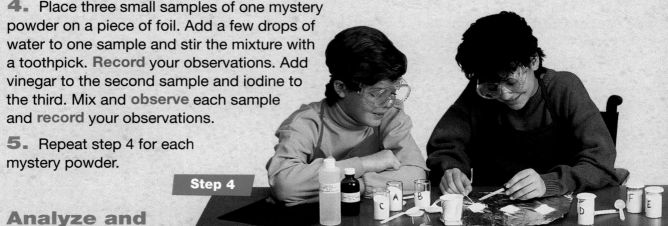

Analyze and Conclude

1. Study your chart and **compare** it with the table above.

2. **Identify** each powder, based on the properties you observed. Write the names in your chart.

INVESTIGATE FURTHER!

EXPERIMENT

Think of a powder you did not use in this activity. Check with your teacher to be sure that your choice is safe. Then have your classmates test your mystery powder. Have them tell which of the six powders studied in this activity is most like your mystery powder.

Activity

"Slime" Time

Look around you. Many objects in your classroom are made of materials that were "invented" by chemists working in laboratories. Plastics and synthetic fibers are good examples of such materials. In this activity you'll make some "slime." Is this a good name for your substance?

Procedure

1. Study samples of water, white glue, food coloring, and borax. **List** them in your *Science Notebook*. **Describe** the appearance of each material and **list** as many properties of each material as you can.

2. Add equal amounts of the water and white glue to a plastic cup. Add a few drops of food coloring and stir the mixture thoroughly with a plastic spoon.

3. **Observe** how the mixture looks. If you wish, you may keep adding more food coloring until the mixture is the color you want.

4. Gradually add the borax to the mixture while you stir it. **Observe** and **record** any changes in the appearance of the mixture.

5. Add borax until no more liquid is visible. Touch the mixture and **describe** how it feels. You can adjust the amount of borax to give your slime exactly the slimy feeling you want it to have.

Step 4

Analyze and Conclude

1. Pick up and handle your slime. **Describe** as many of its properties as you can.

2. **Compare** the properties of your slime to the properties of the materials you mixed together to make it.

3. Think of some possible uses for your slime. **Describe** the uses in your *Science Notebook*.

Polymers and Plastics

Reading Focus What are some organic compounds found in nature, and what are some made by scientists?

SCIENCE TECHNOLOGY & SOCIETY

Scientists once believed that compounds containing carbon could only be produced by living things. Because living things are called organisms, compounds containing carbon were called organic compounds. The study of these compounds was, and still is, called organic chemistry.

Carbon, the Supercombiner

All elements are not created equal. Scientists have identified about 11 million different compounds. Of these, more than 10 million contain carbon.

One of carbon's unique properties is its ability to join, or form bonds, with other atoms. Recall that chemical bonding was described in an earlier section as atoms that are "holding hands." Because of the arrangement of its electrons, a single carbon atom is able to bond or "hold hands" with as many as four other atoms.

This bond-forming ability makes it possible for long chains of carbon atoms to form. Each carbon atom in a chain can also form bonds with atoms of other elements. For example, there are hundreds of ways that compounds can form from the elements carbon and hydrogen.

Not all organic compounds are complex. A molecule of methane (meth'ān), the simplest organic compound, is made up of only five atoms. Models of molecules of methane and two other organic compounds are shown below.

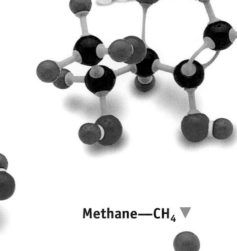

Vitamin C—$C_6H_8O_6$ ▼

Methane—CH_4 ▼

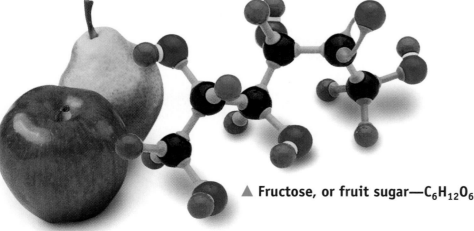

▲ Fructose, or fruit sugar—$C_6H_{12}O_6$

C89

Polymers—Chemical Giants

The next time you sprinkle sugar on your cereal, think of the formula for sugar.

$$C_{12}H_{22}O_{11}$$

Every molecule in those sugar crystals contains 45 atoms! Sounds pretty impressive, doesn't it? Now look at the model of a small part of a protein molecule. Proteins are the building blocks from which your body is made. They are probably the most complex organic compounds found in nature.

Proteins are polymers (päl'ə mərz). A **polymer** is an organic compound made up mainly of a very long chain or chains of carbon compounds. The word *polymer* means "many parts."

Part of a protein molecule ▼

Try to imagine how different your life would be without plastics. Plastics are synthetic polymers. To make a polymer, chemists start with a simple organic molecule. This molecule is one part of the

▲ **Some useful products made of plastic**

polymer. Hundreds or even thousands of these parts are put together to form the carbon chain. At the same time, other molecules are added to the sides of the carbon chain.

The side chains of a polymer determine its properties. For example, side chains can make a polymer hard, flexible, or tough. Just think of all the different kinds of plastics there are and the wide range of properties they exhibit. ■

INVESTIGATE FURTHER!

EXPERIMENT

You can make your own model of a polymer by using paper clips of different sizes and colors, as shown here. Work with a partner to create a paper-clip polymer. When you're finished, describe its properties.

What Chemists Do

Reading Focus What are the two main categories of work that chemists do?

Chemistry is the study of matter—what it's made of and how it behaves. Now think back to the title of this unit—"The Nature of Matter." The unit title could have been "An Introduction to Chemistry." So all this time you have been studying chemistry and doing some of the things chemists do!

Analysis and Synthesis

The things that chemists do can be divided into two large categories—analysis (ə nal'ə sis) and synthesis (sin'thə sis). In simple terms, *analysis* means "taking things apart" and *synthesis* means "putting things together."

Many of the materials you use in everyday life are products of chemical research. Research chemists are constantly inventing and testing new drugs and medicines. The making of polymers, as described earlier, is an excellent example of synthesis.

Types of Chemical Reactions

In conducting their research, chemists observe different types of chemical reactions. Most of those reactions can be classified into one of four major groups—synthesis, decomposition (dē käm pə-zish'ən), single replacement, and double replacement. Take a closer look at these reactions. It might surprise you to know that many of the changes that occur during the activities in this unit involve reactions such as these.

A chemist at work in the laboratory ▼

SYNTHESIS   *Synthesis* means "putting things together." The reaction in which hydrogen gas and oxygen gas combine to produce water is an example of a synthesis reaction in which a water molecule is "put together."

synthesis

DECOMPOSITION   Decomposition involves the breaking down of a substance into simpler substances. In the activity on page C33, sugar is heated, causing it to break down into simpler substances—carbon and water.

decomposition

SINGLE REPLACEMENT   In this type of reaction, one of the elements in a compound is replaced by another element. Such a reaction can be used to coat a piece of metal, such as copper, with a thin layer of another metal, such as silver.

single replacement

DOUBLE REPLACEMENT   In this type of reaction, elements from two different compounds change places, something like two couples changing partners at a dance. Such a reaction produces a solid from two clear liquids in the activity on page C67.

double replacement

Now you know a lot more about matter than you did at the beginning of this unit. You know what matter is made up of. You know what happens when things change. You know what to look for and how to tell whether a change is chemical or physical. And you have an idea of what causes things to change. So congratulations! You are officially a beginning chemist in good standing. ■

INVESTIGATION 3 WRAP-UP

REVIEW

1. What is a polymer?

2. What are four main types of chemical reactions?

CRITICAL THINKING

3. What type of reaction is involved when many small molecules combine to form a polymer?

4. Imagine that a water molecule (H_2O) has undergone decomposition. Explain what happens to the atoms.

REFLECT & EVALUATE

Word Power

Write the letter of the term that best completes each sentence. *Not all terms will be used*.

1. An organic compound made up of a very long chain of carbon compounds is a (an) ____.
2. A substance that changes color when mixed with an acid or a base is a (an) ____.
3. A change from the solid to the liquid state is a (an) ____.
4. One or more new substances are formed in a (an) ____.
5. When an acid reacts with a base, a (an) ____ forms.
6. A negatively charged particle in an atom is a (an) ____.

a. chemical change
b. electron
c. indicator
d. neutron
e. nucleus
f. physical change
g. polymer
h. salt

Check What You Know

Write the term in each pair that correctly completes each sentence.

1. On the pH scale the numbers are higher for solutions that are more (acidic, basic).
2. The number of carbon compounds is more than 10 (thousand, million).
3. A particle with a positive electric charge is a/an (proton, electron).
4. The planetary model of the atom was proposed by (Bohr, Einstein).

Problem Solving

1. Tungsten is an element with 74 protons and 109 neutrons. What is tungsten's atomic number? How many electrons does a tungsten atom have?

2. Sodium (an element) reacts with water (a compound) to produce sodium hydroxide (a compound) and hydrogen gas (an element). What kind of chemical reaction is this? Explain how you know.

Study the photographs. Then use the photographs to explain what happens during a physical change and a chemical change.

Drawing Conclusions

Writers often imply, or hint at, more information than they actually state. They give you clues and expect you to figure out the rest, using what you already know. Suppose an author writes "Ernie the dog awoke suddenly, ran to the door, and stood near it barking furiously." You can conclude that the animal sensed something unusual that alarmed him.

Consider these questions as you draw conclusions.

- What did the author write?
- What do I know?
- What is my conclusion?

Read the paragraphs. Then complete the exercises that follow.

Float or Sink?

Density can be useful in predicting whether an object will sink or float in water. The density of water is 1.0 g/mL. Any material with a density less than 1.0 g/mL will float in water. Anything with a density greater than 1.0 g/mL will sink. How might such information be useful?

Imagine you're going to boil some eggs for breakfast. You want to make sure the eggs aren't spoiled. The density of a fresh egg is about 1.2 g/mL. The density of a spoiled egg is about 0.9 g/mL. If you place an egg in water and it floats, what does this tell you about the egg?

1. **Which statement is a conclusion you can draw from the paragraphs? Write the letter of that statement.**

   a. The density of water is 1.0 g/mL.

   b. Anything with a density greater than 1.0 g/mL will sink.

   c. A spoiled egg will float in water.

   d. A fresh egg will float in water.

2. **What was the most important clue in helping you draw that conclusion?**

 **Line Graph**

The line graph shows the result of an experiment. In the experiment, a quantity of tin was heated.

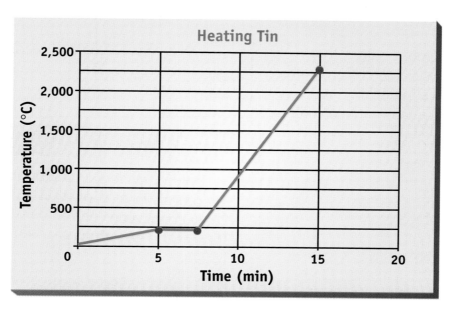

Heating Tin

Use the line graph to complete the exercises.

1. After about 5 minutes of heating, the tin melted. Estimate the temperature at which tin reaches its melting point.

2. About how many minutes did it take for the tin to reach a temperature of 1,200°C?

3. The tin boiled at 2,270°C. About how many minutes did it take for the melted tin to begin to boil?

4. Suppose the experiment began at 2:10 P.M. Estimate the time at which the temperature of the tin reached 1,000°C.

5. What did the line graph look like from 0 to 5 minutes compared to the interval from 5 to 15 minutes? How does the graph show what is happening to the tin as it is being heated?

6. Suppose after 16 minutes the tin is no longer heated. Describe what the graph might look like from 16 minutes to 20 minutes.

C95

WRAP-UP!

On your own, use scientific methods to investigate a question about matter.

THINK LIKE A SCIENTIST

Ask a Question

Pose a question about matter that you would like to investigate. For example, ask, "How does the acidity of rainwater in my area compare with the acidity of distilled water?"

Make a Hypothesis

Suggest a hypothesis that is a possible answer to the question. One hypothesis is that the rainwater in my area is more acidic than distilled water.

Plan and Do a Test

Plan a controlled experiment to compare the acidity of rainwater in your area with the acidity of distilled water. You could start with rainwater, distilled water, several clean containers, and pH paper. Develop a procedure that uses these materials to test the hypothesis. With permission, carry out your experiment. Follow the safety guidelines on pages S14–S15.

Record and Analyze

Observe carefully and record your data accurately. Make repeated observations.

Draw Conclusions

Look for evidence to support the hypothesis or to show that it is false. Draw conclusions about the hypothesis. Repeat the experiment to verify the results.

WRITING IN SCIENCE
Summary

Write a one-paragraph summary of "What Chemists Do," pages C91–C92. Use these guidelines in writing your summary.

- Write one sentence stating the main idea or ideas.
- Include only important details for each main idea.
- Sum up the content in a concluding statement.

Compare your summary with that of a partner.

SCIENCE and MATH TOOLBOX

Using a Microscope

A microscope makes it possible to see very small things by magnifying them. Some microscopes have a set of lenses that magnify objects by different amounts.

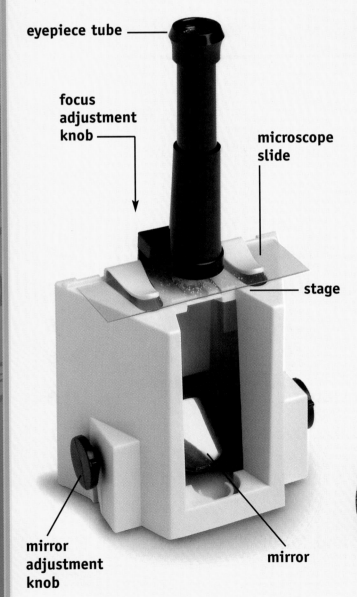

eyepiece tube

focus adjustment knob

microscope slide

stage

mirror adjustment knob

mirror

Examine Some Salt Grains

Handle a microscope carefully; it can break easily. Carry it firmly with both hands and avoid touching the lenses.

1. Turn the mirror toward a source of light. **NEVER** use the Sun as a light source.

2. Place a few grains of salt on the slide. Put the slide on the stage of the microscope.

3. Bring the salt grains into focus. Turn the adjustment knob on the back of the microscope as you look through the eyepiece.

4. Raise the eyepiece tube to increase the magnification; lower it to decrease magnification.

Salt grains magnified one hundred times (100X)

Making a Bar Graph

A bar graph helps you organize and compare data. For example, you might want to make a bar graph to compare weather data for different places.

Make a Bar Graph of Annual Snowfall

For more than 20 years, the cities listed in the table have been recording their yearly snowfall. The table shows the average number of centimeters of snow that the cities receive each year. Use the data in the table to make a bar graph showing the cities' average annual snowfall.

Snowfall	
City	Snowfall (cm)
Atlanta, GA	5
Charleston, SC	1.5
Houston, TX	1
Jackson, MS	3
New Orleans, LA	0.5
Tucson, AZ	3

1. Title your graph. The title should help a reader understand what your graph describes.

2. Choose a scale and mark equal intervals. The vertical scale should include the least value and the greatest value in the set of data.

3. Label the vertical axis *Snowfall (cm)* and the horizontal axis *City*. Space the city names equally.

4. Carefully graph the data. Depending on the interval you choose, some amounts may be between two numbers.

5. Check each step of your work.

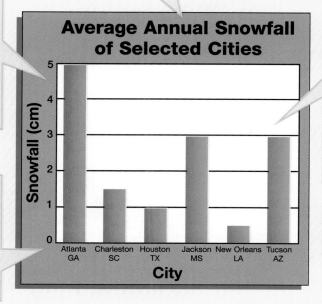

Using a Calculator

After you've made measurements, a calculator can help you analyze your data. Some calculators have a memory key that allows you to save the result of one calculation while you do another.

Add and Divide to Find Percent

The table shows the amount of rain that was collected using a rain gauge in each month of one year. You can use a calculator to help you find the total yearly rainfall. Then you can find the percent of rain that fell during January.

1. Add the numbers. When you add a series of numbers, you need not press the equal sign until the last number is entered. Just press the plus sign after you enter each number (except the last).

2. If you make a mistake while you are entering numbers, press the clear entry (CE/C) key to erase your mistake. Then you can continue entering the rest of the numbers you are adding. If you can't fix your mistake, you can press the (CE/C) key once or twice until the screen shows 0. Then start over.

3. Your total should be 1,131. Now clear the calculator until the screen shows 0. Then divide the rainfall amount for January by the total yearly rainfall (1,131). Press the percent (%) key. Then press the equal sign key.

214 ÷ 1131 % =

The percent of yearly rainfall that fell in January is 18.921309, which rounds to 19%.

Rainfall	
Month	**Rain (mm)**
Jan.	214
Feb.	138
Mar.	98
Apr.	157
May	84
June	41
July	5
Aug.	23
Sept.	48
Oct.	75
Nov.	140
Dec.	108

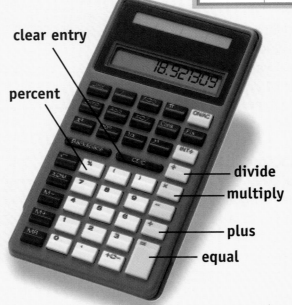

clear entry

percent

divide

multiply

plus

equal

Finding an Average

An average is a way to describe a set of data using one number. For example, you could compare the surface temperature of several stars that are of the same type. You could find the average surface temperature of these stars.

Add and Divide to Find the Average

Suppose scientists found the surface temperature of eight blue-white stars to be those shown in the table. What is the average surface temperature of the stars listed?

Surface Temperature of Selected Blue-white Stars

Blue-white Star	Surface Temperature (°F)
1	7,200
2	6,100
3	6,000
4	6,550
5	7,350
6	6,800
7	7,500
8	6,300

1. First find the sum of the data. Add the numbers in the list.

$$
\begin{array}{r}
7,200 \\
6,100 \\
6,000 \\
6,550 \\
7,350 \\
6,800 \\
7,500 \\
+\ 6,300 \\
\hline
53,800
\end{array}
$$

2. Then divide the sum (53,800) by the number of addends (8).

$$
\begin{array}{r}
6,725 \\
8\,)\overline{53,800} \\
-\ 48 \\
\hline
58 \\
-\ 56 \\
\hline
20 \\
-\ 16 \\
\hline
40 \\
-\ 40 \\
\hline
0
\end{array}
$$

3. $53,800 \div 8 = 6,725$
The average surface temperature of these eight blue-white stars is 6,725°F.

Using a
Tape Measure or Ruler

Tape measures, metersticks, and rulers are tools for measuring length. Scientists use units such as kilometers, meters, centimeters, and millimeters when making length measurements.

Use a Meterstick

1. Work with a partner to find the height of your reach. Stand facing a chalkboard. Reach up as high as you can with one hand.

2. Have your partner use chalk to mark the chalkboard at the highest point of your reach.

3. Use a meterstick to measure your reach to the nearest centimeter. Measure from the floor to the chalk mark. Record the height of your reach.

Use a Tape Measure

1. Use a tape measure to find the circumference of, or distance around, your partner's head. Wrap the tape around your partner's head.

2. Find the line where the tape begins to wrap over itself.

3. Record the distance around your partner's head to the nearest millimeter.

Measuring Volume

A graduated cylinder, a measuring cup, and a beaker are used to measure volume. Volume is the amount of space something takes up. Most of the containers that scientists use to measure volume have a scale marked in milliliters (mL).

Measure the Volume of a Liquid

1. Measure the volume of some juice. Pour the juice into a measuring container.

2. Move your head so that your eyes are level with the top of the juice. Read the scale line that is closest to the surface of the juice. If the surface of the juice is curved up on the sides, look at the lowest point of the curve.

3. Read the measurement on the scale. You can estimate the value between two lines on the scale to obtain a more accurate measurement.

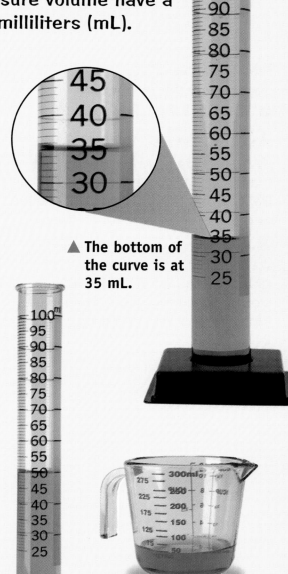

▲ The bottom of the curve is at 35 mL.

This beaker has marks for each 25 mL. ▶

This graduated cylinder has marks for every 1 mL. ▶

▲ This measuring cup has marks for each 25 mL.

Using a Thermometer

A thermometer is used to measure temperature. When the liquid in the tube of a thermometer gets warmer, it expands and moves farther up the tube. Different scales can be used to measure temperature, but scientists usually use the Celsius scale.

Measure the Temperature of a Cold Liquid

1. Half fill a cup with chilled liquid.

2. Hold the thermometer so that the bulb is in the center of the liquid. Be sure that there are no bright lights or direct sunlight shining on the bulb.

3. Wait until you see the liquid in the tube of the thermometer stop moving. Read the scale line that is closest to the top of the liquid in the tube. The thermometer shown reads 21°C (about 70°F).

Using a Balance

A balance is used to measure mass. Mass is the amount of matter in an object. To find the mass of an object, place the object in the left pan of the balance. Place standard masses in the right pan.

Measure the Mass of a Ball

1. Check that the empty pans are balanced, or level with each other. The pointer at the base should be on the middle mark. If it needs to be adjusted, move the slider on the back of the balance a little to the left or right.

2. Place a ball on the left pan. Notice that the pointer moves and that the pans are no longer level with each other. Then add standard masses, one at a time, to the right pan. When the pointer is at the middle mark again, the pans are balanced. Each pan is holding the same amount of matter, and the same mass.

3. Each standard mass is marked to show its number of grams. Add the number of grams marked on the masses in the pan. The total is the mass of the ball in grams.

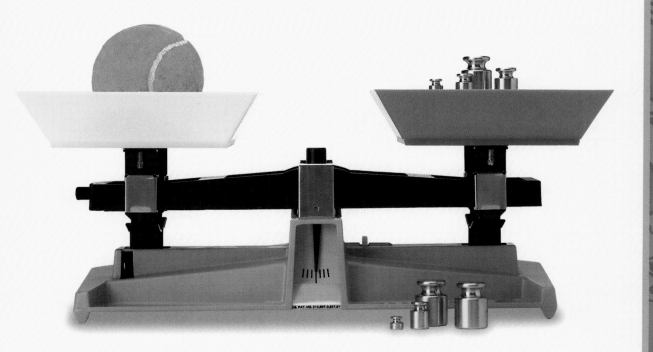

Using an Equation or Formula

Equations and formulas can help you to determine measurements that are not easily made.

Use the Diameter of a Circle to Find Its Circumference

Find the circumference of a circle that has a diameter of 10 cm. To determine the circumference of a circle, use the formula below.

$$C = \pi d$$

$$C = 3.14 \times 10$$

$$C = 31.4 \text{ cm}$$

> π is the symbol for pi. Always use 3.14 as the value for π, unless another value for pi is given.

The circumference of this circle is 31.4 cm.

> The circumference (C) is a measure of the distance around a circle.

10 cm

> The diameter (d) of a circle is a line segment that passes through the center of the circle and connects two points on the circle.

Use Rate and Time to Determine Distance

Suppose an aircraft travels at 772 km/h for 2.5 hours. How many kilometers does the aircraft travel during that time? To determine distance traveled, use the distance formula below.

$$d = rt$$

$$d = 772 \times 2.5$$

$$d = 1{,}930 \text{ km}$$

> d = distance
> r = rate, or the speed at which the aircraft is traveling.
> t = the length of time traveled

The aircraft travels 1,930 km in 2.5 hours.

Making a Chart to Organize Data

A chart can help you record, compare, or classify information.

Organize Properties of Elements

Suppose you collected the data shown at the right. The data presents properties of silver, gold, lead, and iron.

You could organize this information in a chart by classifying the physical properties of each element.

My Data

Silver (Ag) has a density of 10.5 g/cm³. It melts at 961°C and boils at 2,212°C. It is used in dentistry and to make jewelry and electronic conductors.

Gold melts at 1,064°C and boils at 2,966°C. Its chemical symbol is Au. It has a density of 19.3 g/cm³ and is used for jewelry, in coins, and in dentistry.

The melting point of lead (Pb) is 328°C. The boiling point is 1,740°C. It has a density of 11.3 g/cm³. Some uses for lead are in storage batteries, paints, and dyes.

Iron (Fe) has a density of 7.9 g/cm³. It will melt at 1,535°C and boil at 3,000°C. It is used for building materials, in manufacturing, and as a dietary supplement.

Create categories that describe the information you have found.

Give the chart a title that describes what is listed in it.

Properties of Some Elements

Element	Symbol	Density g/cm³	Melting Point (°C)	Boiling Point (°C)	Some Uses
Silver	Ag	10.5	961	2,212	jewelry, dentistry, electric conductors
Gold	Au	19.3	1,064	2,966	jewelry, dentistry, coins
Lead	Pb	11.3	328	1,740	storage batteries, paints, dyes
Iron	Fe	7.9	1,535	3,000	building materials, manufacturing, dietary supplement

Make sure the information is listed accurately in each column.

Reading a Circle Graph

A circle graph shows the whole divided into parts.
You can use a circle graph to compare parts to each
other or to compare parts to the whole.

Read a Circle Graph of Land Area

The whole circle represents the approximate land area of all
of the continents on Earth. The number on each wedge
indicates the land area of each continent. From the graph
you can determine that altogether the land area of the
continents is 148,000,000 square kilometers.

Together
Antarctica and
Australia are
about equal to
the land area of
North America.

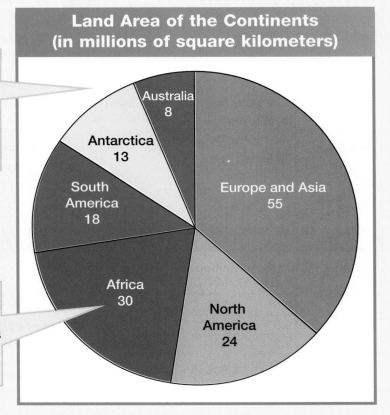

**Land Area of the Continents
(in millions of square kilometers)**

Australia
8

Antarctica
13

South
America
18

Europe and Asia
55

Africa
30

North
America
24

Africa accounts
for more of the
Earth's land area
than South
America.

Making a Line Graph

A line graph is a way to show continuous change over time. You can use the information from a table to make a line graph.

Make a Line Graph of Temperatures

The table shows temperature readings over a 12-hour period at the Dallas–Fort Worth Airport in Texas. This data can also be displayed in a line graph that shows temperature change over time.

Dallas–Fort Worth Airport Temperature	
Hour	Temp. (°C)
6 A.M.	22
7 A.M.	24
8 A.M.	25
9 A.M.	26
10 A.M.	27
11 A.M.	29
12 NOON	31
1 P.M.	32
2 P.M.	33
3 P.M.	34
4 P.M.	35
5 P.M.	35
6 P.M.	34

1. Choose a title. The title should help a reader understand what your graph describes.

2. Choose a scale and mark equal intervals. The vertical scale should include the least value and the greatest value in the set of data.

3. Label the horizontal axis *Time* and the vertical axis *Temperature (°C)*.

4. Write the hours on the horizontal axis. Space the hours equally.

5. Carefully graph the data. Depending on the interval you choose, some temperatures will be between two numbers.

6. Check each step of your work.

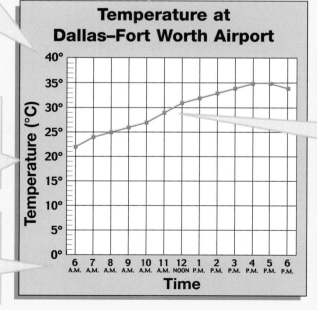

Temperature at Dallas–Fort Worth Airport

Finding
Range, Median, and Mode

You probably know that an average is a way to describe a set of data. Other ways to describe a set of data include range, median, and mode. The data in the table show the speeds at which various animals can run.

Speeds of Animals	
Animal	Speed (km/h)
White-tailed deer	48
Hyena	64
Cheetah	113
Squirrel	19
Zebra	64
Rabbit	56
Human	45

Finding the Range

The **range** can tell you if the data is spread far apart or clustered. To find the range, subtract the least number from the greatest number in a set of data.

$$113 - 19 = 94$$

The difference, or range, of the data is 94.

19 45 48 56 64 64 113

Finding the Median

The **median** is the middle number or the average of the two middle numbers when the data is arranged in order. The middle or median of the data set is 56.

Finding the Mode

The **mode** is the number or numbers that occur most often in a set of data. Sometimes there is no mode or more than one mode. The number that occurs most often is 64.

Using a Spring Scale

A spring scale is used to measure force. You can use a spring scale to find the weight of an object in newtons. You can also use the scale to measure other forces.

Measure the Weight of an Object

1. Place the object in a net bag and hang it from the hook on the bottom of the spring scale. Or, if possible, hang the object directly from the hook.

2. Slowly lift the scale by the handle at the top. Be sure the object to be weighed continues to hang from the hook.

3. Wait until the indicator inside the clear tube of the spring scale has stopped moving. Read the number next to the indicator. This number is the weight of the object in newtons.

Measure Friction

1. Hang the object from the hook at the bottom of the spring scale. Use a piece of string to connect the hook and object if needed.

2. Gently pull the handle at the top of the scale parallel to the floor. When the object starts to move, read the number of newtons next to the indicator on the scale. This number is the force of friction between the floor and the object as you drag the object.

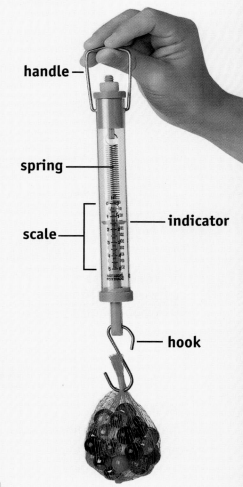

handle

spring

scale

indicator

hook

MEASUREMENTS

Volume
1 L of sports drink is a little more than 1 qt.

Area
A basketball court covers about 4,700 ft². It covers about 435 m².

Mass and Weight
A basketball has a mass of about 650 g. It weighs about $1\frac{1}{2}$ lb.

Metric Measures

Temperature
Ice melts at 0 degrees Celsius (°C)

Water freezes at 0°C

Water boils at 100°C

Length and Distance
1,000 meters (m) = 1 kilometer (km)

100 centimeters (cm) = 1 m

10 millimeters (mm) = 1 cm

Force
1 newton (N) =
    1 kilogram x meter/second/second
    (kg x m/s²)

Volume
1 cubic meter (m³) = 1 m x 1 m x 1 m

1 cubic centimeter (cm³) =
    1 cm x 1 cm x 1 cm

1 liter (L) = 1,000 milliliters (mL)

1 cm³ = 1 mL

Area
1 square kilometer (km²) = 1 km x 1 km

1 hectare = 10,000 m²

Mass
1,000 grams (g) = 1 kilogram (kg)

1,000 milligrams (mg) = 1 g

Temperature
The temperature at an indoor basketball game might be 25°C, which is 77°F.

Length/ Distance
A basketball rim is about 10 ft high, or a little more than 3 m from the floor.

Customary Measures

Temperature

Ice melts at 32 degrees Fahrenheit (°F)

Water freezes at 32°F

Water boils at 212°F

Length and Distance

12 inches (in.) = 1 foot (ft)

3 ft = 1 yard (yd)

5,280 ft = 1 mile (mi)

Weight

16 ounces (oz) = 1 pound (lb)

2,000 pounds = 1 ton (T)

Volume of Fluids

8 fluid ounces (fl oz) = 1 cup (c)

2 c = 1 pint (pt)

2 pt = 1 quart (qt)

4 qt = 1 gallon (gal)

Metric and Customary Rates

km/h = kilometers per hour

m/s = meters per second

mph = miles per hour

GLOSSARY

Pronunciation Key

Symbol	Key Words
a	cat
ā	ape
ä	cot, car
e	ten, berry
ē	me
i	fit, here
ī	ice, fire
ō	go
ô	fall, for
oi	oil
ơơ	look, pull
o͞o	tool, rule
ou	out, crowd
u	up
ʉ	fur, shirt
ə	a in ago
	e in agent
	i in pencil
	o in atom
	u in circus
b	bed
d	dog
f	fall

Symbol	Key Words
g	get
h	help
j	jump
k	kiss, call
l	leg
m	meat
n	nose
p	put
r	red
s	see
t	top
v	vat
w	wish
y	yard
z	zebra
ch	chin, arch
ŋ	ring, drink
sh	she, push
th	thin, truth
th	then, father
zh	measure

A heavy stress mark (′) is placed after a syllable that gets a heavy, or primary, stress, as in **picture** (pik′chər).

A

abyssal plain (ə bis′əl plān) The broad, flat ocean bottom. (E34) The *abyssal plain* covers nearly half of Earth's surface.

acceleration (ak sel ər ā′shən) The rate at which velocity changes over time. (F21) The spacecraft's *acceleration* increased as it soared into the air.

acid (as′id) A compound that turns blue litmus paper to red and forms a salt when it reacts with a base. (C81) *Acids* have a sour taste.

action force The initial force exerted in a force-pair. (F90) When you push against something, you are applying an *action force.*

active transport The process by which the cell uses energy to move materials through the cell membrane. (A17) Food molecules are moved into a cell by *active transport.*

aftershock A less powerful shock following the principal shock of an earthquake. (B56) Many *aftershocks* shook the ground in the days after the major earthquake.

algae (al′jē) Any of various mostly single-celled plantlike protists. (A34) Diatoms and seaweed are kinds of *algae.*

alloy (al′oi) A solution of two or more metals. (C59) Bronze is an *alloy* of copper and tin.

antibiotic (an tī bī ät′ik) A substance, often produced by microbes or fungi, that can stop the growth and reproduction of bacteria. (A57) Doctors prescribe *antibiotics* to treat various diseases.

antibody (an′ti bäd ē) A protein produced in the blood that destroys or weakens bacteria and viruses. (A57) *Antibodies* are produced in response to infection.

aquaculture (ak′wə kul chər) The raising of water plants and animals for human use or consumption. (E78) Raising catfish on a catfish "farm" is a form of *aquaculture.*

archaeologist (är kē äl′ə jist) A scientist who studies ancient cultures by digging up evidence of human life from the past. (B90) *Archaeologists* discovered human remains in the ancient city of Pompeii.

asexual reproduction (ā sek′shσο al rē prə duk′ shən) Reproduction involving a cell or cells from one parent that results in offspring exactly like the parent. (D10) The division of an amoeba into two cells is an example of *asexual reproduction.*

asthenosphere (as then′ə sfir) The layer of Earth below the lithosphere; the upper part of the mantle. (B36) The *asthenosphere* contains hot, partially melted rock with plasticlike properties.

astronomical unit A unit of measurement equal to the distance from Earth to the Sun. (F9) Pluto is 39.3 *astronomical units* (A.U.) from the Sun.

atom The smallest particle of an element that has the chemical properties of that element. (C35) An *atom* of sodium differs from an *atom* of chlorine.

atomic number (ə täm′ik num′bər) The number of protons in the nucleus of an atom. (C73) The *atomic number* of oxygen is 8.

bacteria (bak tir′ē ə) Monerans that feed on dead organic matter or on living things. (A49) Diseases such as pneumonia and tuberculosis are caused by *bacteria*.

base A compound that turns red litmus paper blue and that forms a salt when it reacts with an acid. (C81) *Bases* have a slippery feel.

benthos (ben′thäs) All the plants and animals that live on the ocean bottom. (E25) The *benthos* group include oysters, crabs, and coral.

blue-green bacteria (blo͞o grēn bak tir′ē ə) Monerans that contain chlorophyll. (A49) Like plants, *blue-green bacteria* carry out photosynthesis and make their own food.

budding A form of asexual reproduction in which a new individual develops from a bump, or bud, on the body of the parent. (D13) Some one-celled organisms, such as yeast, reproduce by *budding.*

buoyancy (boi′ən sē) The upward force exerted by a fluid on objects submerged in the fluid. (F121) Objects float better in salt water than in fresh water because salt water has greater *buoyancy.*

caldera (kal der′ə) A large circular depression, or basin, at the top of a volcano. (B102) The eruption formed a *caldera* that later became a lake.

cast fossil (kast fäs′əl) A fossil formed when minerals from rock move into and harden inside the space left by a decaying organism. (D55) *Cast fossils* of shells can provide information about the animals from which the fossils formed.

cell The basic unit that makes up all living things. (A9) The human body is made up of trillions of *cells.*

cell differentiation (sel dif ər en-shē ā′shən) The development of cells into different and specialized cell types. (A25) Through *cell differentiation*, plant cells and animal cells develop into tissues.

cell membrane (sel mem′brān) The structure that surrounds and encloses a cell and controls the movement of substances into and out of the cell. (A10) The *cell membrane* shrank when the cell was placed in salt water.

cell respiration (sel res pə rā′shən) The process in cells in which oxygen is used to release stored energy by breaking down sugar molecules. (A19) The process of *cell respiration* provides energy for a cell's activities.

cell theory A theory that explains the structure of all living things. (A10) The *cell theory* states that all living things are made up of cells.

cell wall The rigid structure surrounding the cells of plants, monerans, and some protists. (A10) The *cell wall* gives a cell its rigid shape.

chemical change A change in matter that results in one or more new substances with new properties. (C69) A *chemical change* occurs when wood burns and forms gases and ash.

chemical formula A group of symbols and numbers that shows the elements that make up a compound. (C40) The *chemical formula* for carbon dioxide is CO_2.

chemical properties Characteristics of matter that describe how it changes when it reacts with other matter. (C34) The ability to burn is a *chemical property* of paper.

chemical symbol One or two letters used to stand for the name of an element. (C36) Ca is the *chemical symbol* for calcium.

20
Ca
Calcium

chloroplast (klôr′ə plast) A tiny green organelle that contains chlorophyll and is found in plant cells and some protist cells. (A10) The chlorophyll inside a *chloroplast* enables a plant cell to capture solar energy.

chromosome (krō′mə sōm) A threadlike structure in the nucleus of a cell; it carries the genes that determine the traits an offspring inherits from its parent or parents. (A10, D22) Most cells in the human body contain 23 pairs of *chromosomes*.

cinder cone A kind of volcano, usually steep-sloped, that is formed from layers of cinders, which are sticky bits of volcanic material. (B86) *Cinder cones* result from explosive eruptions.

communicable disease (kə myoo′ni-kə bəl di zēz) A disease that can be passed from one individual to another. (A58) Bacteria, which are easily passed from organism to organism, are the cause of many *communicable diseases*.

competition (käm pə tish′ən) The struggle among organisms for available resources. (D77) *Competition* among members of a species is a factor in evolution.

composite cone (kəm päz′it kōn)
A kind of volcano formed when explosive eruptions of sticky lava alternate with quieter eruptions of volcanic rock bits. (B89) Mount Vesuvius is a *composite cone* in southern Italy.

compound (käm′pound) A substance made up of two or more elements that are chemically combined. (C34) Water is a *compound* made up of hydrogen and oxygen.

condensation (kän dən sā′shən)
The change of state from a gas to a liquid. (C28) The *condensation* of water vapor can form droplets of water on the outside of a cold glass.

continental edge (kän tə nent′′l ej)
The point at which the continental shelf, which surrounds each continent, begins to angle sharply downward. (E33) Beyond the *continental edge* the ocean increases rapidly in depth.

continental rise The lower portion of the continental slope, extending to the deep ocean floor. (E33) The *continental rise* slopes downward to the deepest part of the ocean.

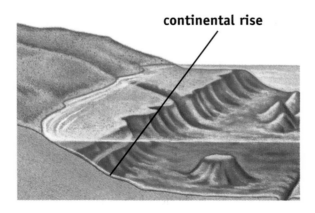

continental rise

continental shelf The gently sloping shelf of land extending from the shoreline to the continental edge. (E32) The *continental shelf* can extend hundreds of miles out into the ocean.

continental slope The steep clifflike drop from the continental edge to the deep ocean floor. (E33) The *continental slope* connects the continental shelf with the ocean bottom.

controlled experiment A test of a hypothesis in which the setups are identical in all ways except one. (S7) In the *controlled experiment*, one beaker of water contained salt.

convection (kən vek′shən) The process by which heat energy is transferred through liquids or gases. (B37) The air was heated by *convection*.

convection current The path along which energy is transferred during convection. (B37) Scientists think that *convection currents* in the mantle cause Earth's tectonic plates to move.

convergent boundary (kən vʉr′jənt boun′də rē) A place where the plates that make up Earth's crust and upper mantle collide or come together. (B38) Layers of rock may bend or break at a *convergent boundary*.

Coriolis effect (kôr ē ō′lis e fekt′)
The tendency of a body or fluid moving across Earth's surface to have a curving motion due to Earth's rotation. (E54) The *Coriolis effect* causes air and water currents to move clockwise in the Northern Hemisphere.

crest The top of a wave. (E63) The *crest* of the wave seemed to tower over the surfer.

crust The thin outer layer of Earth. (B19) Earth's *crust* varies in thickness from 5 km to 48 km.

current Great rivers of water moving through the ocean. (E53) The strong *current* pulled the boat away from shore.

cytoplasm (sīt'ō plaz əm) The watery gel inside a cell. (A11) Various organelles, including vacuoles and mitochondria, are found inside the *cytoplasm* of a cell.

deceleration (dē sel ər ā'shən) A decrease in speed over time. (F23) Air resistance can cause the *deceleration* of objects.

density The amount of mass in a given volume of matter. (C13) Lead has a greater *density* than aluminum.

desalination (dē sal ə nā'shən) A process for obtaining fresh water from salt water by removing the salt. (E78) A few countries operate *desalination* plants, which obtain fresh water from ocean water.

diatom (dī'ə täm) A microscopic, one-celled algae with a glasslike cell wall. (A34) A single liter of sea water may contain millions of *diatoms* of various kinds.

diffusion (di fyōō'zhən) The movement of substances from an area of greater concentration to an area of lesser concentration. (A16) Oxygen can pass in and out of cells by *diffusion*.

divergent boundary (dī vʉr'jənt boun'də rē) A place where the plates that make up Earth's crust and upper mantle move away from one another. (B38) Most *divergent boundaries* are found on the floor of the ocean.

dome mountain A mountain formed when magma lifts Earth's surface, creating a broad dome, or bulge. (B45) Pikes Peak in Colorado is a *dome mountain.*

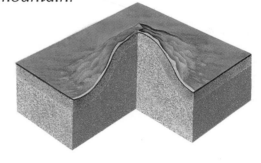

domesticated (dō mes'ti kāt əd) Tamed or bred to serve people's purposes. (D68) People breed *domesticated* animals such as horses for transportation and other uses.

dominant trait (däm'ə nənt trāt) A trait that will be expressed if it is inherited. (D43) Gregor Mendel found that tallness was a *dominant trait* in pea plants.

drag A force that resists forward motion through a fluid; it operates in the direction opposite to thrust. (F109) The air causes *drag* on an airplane.

earthquake A shaking or movement of Earth's surface, caused by the release of stored energy along a fault. (B56) Many *earthquakes* occur near the boundaries between tectonic plates.

electron (ē lek′trän) A negatively charged particle in an atom. (C71) The number of *electrons* in an atom usually equals the number of protons.

element (el′ə mənt) A substance that cannot be broken down into any other substance by ordinary chemical means. (C34) Oxygen, hydrogen, copper, iron, and carbon are *elements*.

endangered species A species of animal or plant whose number has become so small that the species is in danger of becoming extinct. (D25) The black-footed ferret is an *endangered species* that is found in North America.

epicenter (ep′i sent ər) The point on Earth's surface directly above an earthquake's point of origin, or focus. (B63) The *epicenter* of the earthquake was 2 km north of the city.

era (ir′a) One of the major divisions of geologic time. (D57) Many kinds of mammals developed during the Cenozoic *Era*.

ethanol (eth′ə nôl) A kind of alcohol used to make medicines, food products, and various other items. (A40) *Ethanol* is a flammable liquid that can be used as a fuel.

evaporation (ē vap ə rā′shən) The change of state from a liquid to a gas. (C27) Heat from the Sun caused the *evaporation* of the water.

evolution (ev ə lōō′shən) The development of new species from earlier species over time. (D56) According to the theory of *evolution*, the plants and animals alive today descended from organisms that lived millions of years ago.

extinct (ek stiŋkt′) No longer in existence; having no living descendant. (D25) Dinosaurs and mammoths are both *extinct*.

extinction (ek stiŋk′shən) The disappearance of species from Earth. (D60) Scientists do not agree about what caused the *extinction* of the dinosaurs.

fault A break in rock along which rock slabs have moved. (B63) The shifting of Earth's tectonic plates can produce a *fault*, along which earthquakes may occur.

fault-block mountain A mountain formed when masses of rock move up or down along a fault. (B45) Mountains in the Great Rift Valley of Africa are *fault-block mountains.*

fermentation (fŭr mən tā'shən) A chemical change in which an organism breaks down sugar to produce carbon dioxide and alcohol or lactic acid. (A19) The action of yeast caused *fermentation* in the sugary liquid.

fertilization (fŭr tə li zā'shən) The process by which a sperm and an egg unite to form a cell that will develop into a new individual. (D24) In humans, *fertilization* produces a cell containing 46 chromosomes, half from the female parent and half from the male parent.

fetch (fech) The distance the wind blows over open water. (E64) The longer the *fetch*, the bigger the waves become.

first law of motion The concept that objects at rest tend to remain at rest and objects in motion tend to remain in motion, traveling at a constant speed and in the same direction. (F59) According to the *first law of motion*, a stationary object will stay in place unless some force causes the object to move.

fission (fish'ən) A method of asexual reproduction in which a parent cell divides to form two identical new cells. (A32, D10) Many one-celled organisms, such as amoebas, reproduce by *fission.*

focus (fō'kəs) The point, or place, at which an earthquake begins. (B63) The *focus* of the earthquake was about 20 km beneath Earth's surface.

folded mountain A mountain formed when two tectonic plates collide. (B43) The Alps and the Himalayas are *folded mountains.*

force A push or a pull. (F33) The *force* of friction caused the rolling wagon to slow and then stop.

fossil (fäs'əl) The remains or traces of a living thing, usually preserved in rock. (D54) *Fossils* are usually found in sedimentary rock.

freezing The change of state from a liquid to a solid. (C28) The *freezing* of water occurs at 0°C.

friction (frik'shən) A force that resists motion between two surfaces that are in contact with each other. (F73) *Friction* keeps a car's tires from slipping off the road.

fungi (fun'jī) Organisms that feed on dead organisms or that are parasitic. (A41) Most *fungi* attach to and grow on organic matter.

gene (jēn) One of the units that make up a chromosome; genes determine the traits an offspring inherits from its parent or parents. (D33) Half of your *genes* come from your mother, and half come from your father.

gene splicing (jēn spli′siŋ) A process by which genes are manipulated to alter the function or nature of an organism, usually by being transferred from one organism to another. (D45) Through *gene splicing*, scientists have transferred a gene for making insulin from one organism to another.

genetic engineering (jə net′ik en-jə nir′iŋ) The process by which genes are manipulated to bring about biological change in species. (D46) Using *genetic engineering* techniques, scientists have successfully combined DNA from different organisms.

gravity (grav′i tē) The force that pulls objects toward Earth; also, the attractive force exerted by a body or an object on other bodies or objects. (F33) *Gravity* causes a ball to fall to the ground after it is thrown into the air.

heat Energy that flows from warmer to cooler regions of matter. (C26) *Heat* can cause matter to change from one state to another.

hot spot A place deep within Earth's mantle that is extremely hot and contains a chamber of magma. (B100) Magma rising from a *hot spot* can break through Earth's crust to form a volcano.

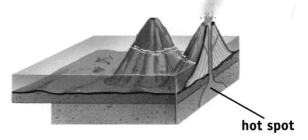

hot spot

hypothesis (hī päth′ə sis) An idea about or explanation of how or why something happens. (S6) The *hypothesis* about the expanding universe has been supported by evidence gathered by astronomers.

immune system (im myo͞on′ sis′təm) The body system that defends the body against diseases. (A56) The *immune system* produces antibodies to fight disease.

incomplete dominance (in kəm-plēt′ däm′ə nəns) The expression of both genes (traits) in a pair, producing a blended effect. (D44) A plant with pink flowers, produced by crossing a plant having red flowers with a plant having white flowers, is an example of *incomplete dominance.*

indicator (in′di kāt ər) A substance that changes color when mixed with an acid or a base. (C81) Paper treated with an *indicator* is used to test whether a compound is an acid or a base.

inertia (in ʉr′shə) The tendency of an object to remain at rest if at rest, or if in motion, to remain in motion in the same direction. (F59) *Inertia* results in passengers in a car moving forward when the driver applies the brakes.

inherited trait (in her′it əd trāt) A trait that is passed on from parents to offspring through genes. (D32) Eye color is an *inherited trait.*

ion (ī′ən) An electrically charged atom. (C73) *Ions* form when atoms lose or gain electrons. Sodium chloride is made up of sodium *ions* and chlorine *ions.*

island arc A chain of volcanoes formed from magma that rises as a result of an oceanic plate sinking into the mantle. (B94) The Philippine Islands are part of an *island arc.*

kinetic energy (ki net′ik en′ər jē) Energy of motion. (C25) A ball rolling down a hill has *kinetic energy.*

lava (lä′və) Magma that flows out onto Earth's surface from a volcano. (B85) Flaming *lava* poured down the sides of the volcanic mountain.

law of conservation of momentum The principle that states that momentum can be transferred but cannot be lost. (F84) The *law of conservation of momentum* explains why the momentum resulting from the collision of two objects equals the total momentum of the objects before they collided.

learned trait A trait that is not passed on in DNA, but instead is acquired through learning or experience. (D34) The ability to speak Spanish is a *learned trait.*

lift The upward force, resulting from differences in air pressure above and below an airplane's wings, that causes the airplane to rise. (F109) Increasing the size of an airplane's wings increases *lift.*

lithosphere (lith′ō sfir) The solid, rocky layer of Earth, including the crust and top part of the mantle. (B36) The *lithosphere* is about 100 km in thickness.

magma (mag′mə) The hot, molten rock deep inside Earth. (B84) The *magma* rose from the underground chamber through the volcano.

magnetic field The space around a magnet within which the force of the magnet is exerted. (B26) The magnet attracted all the iron filings within its *magnetic field.*

magnetic reversal (mag net'ik ri-vʉr'səl) The switching or changing of Earth's magnetic poles such that the north magnetic pole becomes located at the south magnetic pole's position and vice versa. (B26) Scientists have found evidence of *magnetic reversals* in layers of rock along the ocean floor.

magnitude (mag'nə to͞od) The force or strength of an earthquake. (B57) *Magnitude* is a measure of the amount of energy released by an earthquake.

mantle The layer of Earth between the crust and the core. (B19) The *mantle* is made up of a thick layer of rock.

mass The amount of matter in an object. (C10, F32) A large rock has more *mass* than a pebble.

matter Anything that has mass and volume. (C10, F32) Rocks, water, and air are three kinds of *matter*.

meiosis (mī ō'sis) The process of cell division by which sex cells receive half the number of chromosomes as other body cells. (D22) Because of *meiosis*, a sex cell in a human has only 23 chromosomes instead of 46.

melt To change state from a solid to a liquid. (C27) The icicles began to *melt*.

metric system A system of measurement based on a few defined units and in which larger and smaller units are related by powers of 10. (F11) In the *metric system*, a centimeter is 10 times longer than a millimeter.

mid-ocean ridge A chain of mountains on the ocean floor. (B27, E34) New ocean floor forms at the *mid-ocean ridge*.

mitochondria (mīt ō kän'drē ə) Cell organelles in which energy is released from food. (A11) The more *mitochondria* a cell has, the more energy it can release from food.

mitosis (mī tō'sis) The process in which one cell divides to form two identical new cells. (A23) The new cells that are formed by *mitosis* have the same number of chromosomes as the parent cell.

mixture A combination of two or more substances that can be separated by physical means. (C34) This jar contains a *mixture* of colored beads.

model Something used or made to represent an object or to describe how a process takes place. (C71) The plastic *model* showed the structure of the heart.

mold fossil (mōld fäs'əl) A fossil consisting of a hollowed space in the shape of an organism or one of its parts. (D54) Footprints of animals left in mud that dried in the sun became a type of *mold fossil*.

molecule (mäl'i kyo͞ol) A particle made up of a group of atoms that are chemically bonded. (C39) A *molecule* of water contains two hydrogen atoms and one oxygen atom.

momentum (mō men'təm) A property of a moving object, calculated by multiplying the object's mass by its velocity. (F82) The train gathered *momentum* as its speed increased.

moneran (ma nir'ən) Any one-celled organism in which the cell does not have a nucleus. (A48) Bacteria are *monerans.*

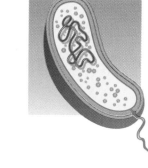

multicellular (mul ti sel'yoo lər) Made up of more than one cell. (A32) Some protists are *multicellular.*

mutation (myoo tā'shən) A change in a gene's DNA that can result in a new characteristic, or trait. (D74) Certain *mutations* have helped species survive in their environment.

natural selection (nach'ər əl sə-lek'shən) The process by which those living things that have characteristics that allow them to adapt to their environment tend to live longest and produce the most offspring, passing on these favorable characteristics to their offspring. (D73) *Natural selection* helps explain why certain characteristics become common while others die out.

neap tide (nēp tīd) The tide occurring at the first and third quarters of the Moon, when the difference in level between high and low tide is smallest. (E69) *Neap tides* occur twice each month.

nekton (nek'tän) All the free-swimming animals that live in the ocean. (E25) The *nekton* group includes such active animals as fish, octopuses, and whales.

neutralization (noo trə lī zā'shən) The reaction between an acid and a base. (C83) *Neutralization* produces water and a salt.

neutron (noo'trän) A particle in the nucleus of an atom that has no electric charge. (C71) The mass of a *neutron* is about equal to the mass of a proton.

newton (noo'tən) A unit used to measure force in the metric system. (F67) A *newton* is the force needed to accelerate a one-kilogram object by one meter per second every second.

nuclear fission (noo'klē ər fish'ən) The splitting of the nucleus of an atom, releasing great amounts of energy. (C77) Bombarding a nucleus with neutrons can cause *nuclear fission.*

nuclear membrane The structure that surrounds the nucleus and controls what substances move into and out of the nucleus. (A11) The *nuclear membrane* appears to be solid, but it actually has tiny holes through which materials can pass.

nucleus (nōō'klē əs) 1. The control center of a cell. (A11) The *nucleus* contains the cell's genetic information. 2. The dense, central part of an atom. (C71) The *nucleus* is made up of protons and neutrons and contains nearly all of an atom's mass.

organ A part of a multicellular organism made up of a group of tissues that work together to perform a certain function. (A25) The heart, stomach, brain, and the lungs are *organs* of the human body.

organ system A group of organs that work together to perform one or more functions. (A26) The bones are part of the *organ system* that supports the body.

osmosis (äs mō'sis) The diffusion of water through a membrane. (A16) Water enters and leaves a cell through the process of *osmosis*.

paleontologist (pā lē ən täl'ə jist) A scientist who studies fossils. (D56) A team of *paleontologists* discovered the remains of a dinosaur.

Pangaea (pan jē'ə) A supercontinent that existed about 200 million years ago. (B9) *Pangaea* broke apart into several continents.

period 1. A division of geologic time that is a subdivision of an era. (D57) The Jurassic *Period* is part of the Mesozoic Era. 2. The time it takes for two successive waves to pass the same point. (E63) The *period* for the ocean waves was about ten seconds.

petrification (pe tri fi kā'shən) The changing of the hard parts of a dead organism to stone. (D55) Fossils of trees have been preserved by *petrification*.

photosynthesis (fōt ō sin'thə sis) The process by which green plants and other producers use light energy to make food. (A18, E24) In *photosynthesis*, plant cells use light energy to make sugar from carbon dioxide and water.

physical change A change in size, shape, or state of matter, with no new kind of matter being formed. (C68) The freezing of water into ice cubes is an example of a *physical change*.

physical properties Characteristics of matter that can be measured or detected by the senses. (C34) Color is a *physical property* of minerals.

phytoplankton (fīt ō plaŋk'tən) The group of usually microscopic plantlike protists that live near the surface of the ocean. (E10) *Phytoplankton* drifts with the ocean currents.

plankton (plaŋk'tən) The group of organisms, generally microscopic in size, that float or drift near the ocean surface. (A34, E10) *Plankton* is a source of food for fish.

plate boundary A place where the plates that make up Earth's crust and upper mantle either move together or apart or else move past one another. (B20) Earthquakes occur along *plate boundaries.*

pollution The contamination of the environment with waste materials or other unwanted substances. (E89) Dangerous chemicals dumped into the ocean are one source of *pollution.*

polymer (päl'ə mər) An organic compound consisting of large molecules formed from many smaller, linked molecules. (C90) Proteins are *polymers.*

protist (prōt'ist) Any of a large group of mostly single-celled, microscopic organisms that have traits of plants, animals, or both. (A32) Parameciums and algae are *protists.*

proton (prō'tän) A positively charged particle found in the nucleus of an atom. (C71) The atomic number of an atom equals the number of *protons* in the atom's nucleus.

protozoan (prō tō zō'ən) A protist that has animal-like traits. (A32) A paramecium is a *protozoan.*

radioactive element (rā dē ō ak'tiv el'ə mənt) An element made up of atoms whose nuclei break down, or decay, into nuclei of other atoms. (C76) As the nucleus of a *radioactive element* decays, energy and particles are released.

reaction force The force exerted in response to an action force. (F90) A *reaction force* is equal in strength to an action force but opposite in direction to the action force.

recessive trait (ri ses'iv trāt) A trait that will not be expressed if paired with a dominant trait. (D43) In his experiments with pea plants, Gregor Mendel learned that shortness was a *recessive trait.*

reproduction (rē prə duk' shən) The process by which organisms produce more of their own kind. (D10) *Reproduction* ensures the survival of the species.

Richter scale (rik'tər skāl) A scale of numbers by which the magnitude of earthquakes is measured. (B56) Each increase of 1.0 on the *Richter scale* represents an increase of about 30 times the energy released by an earthquake.

rifting (rift'iŋ) The process by which magma rises to fill the gap between two plates that are moving apart. (B106) *Rifting* in eastern Africa may split the continent into two parts.

salinity (sə lin′ə tē) The total amount of dissolved salts in ocean water. (E9) The *salinity* of the ocean varies in different parts of the world.

salt A compound that can be formed when an acid reacts with a base. (C83) When vinegar and baking soda interact, they produce a *salt* and water.

saprophyte (sap′rə fīt) An organism that lives on dead or decaying matter. (A42) Molds are *saprophytes*.

sea-floor spreading The process by which new ocean floor is continually being formed as magma rises to the surface and hardens into rock. (B28) *Sea-floor spreading* occurs as magma fills the space between separating plates.

seamount (sē′mount) An underwater mountain that formed from a volcano. (E34) Thousands of *seamounts* rise from the floor of the Pacific.

second law of motion The concept that an object that is at rest or in motion will not change its condition unless something causes the change. (F65) A gust of wind blowing an open umbrella out of your hands illustrates the *second law of motion*.

seismograph (sīz′mə graf) An instrument that records the intensity, duration, and nature of earthquake waves. (B72) Scientists use information from *seismographs* to determine the location of earthquakes.

seismometer (sīz mäm′ə tər) An instrument that detects and records Earth's movements. (B96) Data from the *seismometer* suggested that a volcanic eruption might soon occur.

selective breeding Breeding of living things to produce offspring with certain desired characteristics. (D68) People have used *selective breeding* to produce domesticated animals.

sex cell A female or male reproductive cell; an egg cell or sperm cell. (D22) Reproduction can occur when *sex cells* unite.

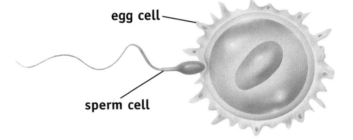

egg cell

sperm cell

sexual reproduction Reproduction that involves the joining of a male sex cell and a female sex cell. (D22) Most animals and plants produce offspring through *sexual reproduction*.

shield cone A kind of volcanic cone that is large and gently sloped and that is formed when lava flows quietly from a crack in the Earth's crust. (B87) Mauna Loa, a *shield cone* in Hawaii, is the largest volcano on Earth.

solute (säl′yo͞ot) The material present in the smaller amount in a solution; the substance dissolved in a solution. (C57) If you dissolve sugar in water, sugar is the *solute*.

solution A mixture in which the different particles are spread evenly throughout the mixture. (C57) Dissolving salt in water makes a *solution.*

solvent (säl′vənt) The material present in the greater amount in a solution; the substance in a solution, usually a liquid, that dissolves another substance. (C57) If you mix sugar and water, water is the *solvent.*

speed The distance traveled in a certain amount of time; rate of movement. (F16) The truck was moving at a *speed* of 40 mph.

spore A reproductive cell that can develop into a new organism. (A41) Ferns and mushrooms produce *spores.*

spring tide An extremely high tide or low tide occurring at or just after the new moon and full moon. (E69) At the time of a *spring tide*, both the Sun and the Moon are in line with Earth.

state of matter Any of the three forms that matter may take: solid, liquid, or gas. (C20) Water's *state of matter* depends on its temperature.

substance (sub′stəns) Matter that always has the same makeup and properties, wherever it may be found. (C34) Elements and compounds are *substances.*

tectonic plate (tek tän′ik plāt) One of the slabs that make up Earth's crust and upper mantle; also called *tectonic plate.* (B19) Some of Earth's *tectonic plates* carry continents.

temperature A measure of the average kinetic energy of the particles in matter. (C26) Water *temperature* rises as the motion of water molecules increases.

theory (thē′ ə re) A hypothesis that is supported by a lot of evidence and is widely accepted by scientists. (S9) The Big Bang *Theory* offers an explanation for the origin of the universe.

theory of continental drift A theory that states that the continents formed a single landmass at one time in the past and have drifted over time to their present positions. (B10) The *theory of continental drift* was first suggested by Alfred Wegener.

theory of plate tectonics The theory that Earth's lithosphere is broken into enormous slabs, or plates, that are in motion. (B19) Scientists use the *theory of plate tectonics* to explain how Earth's continents drift.

third law of motion The concept that for every action force there is an equal and opposite reaction force. (F90) When you watch someone's feet bouncing off a trampoline, you see the *third law of motion* at work.

thrust (thrust) The push or driving force that causes an airplane, rocket, or other object to move forward. (F108) *Thrust* can be produced by a spinning propeller or by a jet engine.

tide The daily rise and fall of the level of the ocean or other large body of water, caused by the gravitational attraction of the Moon and the Sun. (E68) As the *tide* came in, we moved our blanket back from the water's edge.

tiltmeter (tilt′mēt ər) An instrument that measures any change in the slope of an area. (B96) Scientists use *tiltmeters* to note any bulges that form in a mountain's slopes.

tissue A group of similar, specialized cells working together to carry out the same function. (A25) Muscle *tissue* contains cells that contract.

toxin (täks′in) A chemical poison that is harmful to the body. (A54) *Toxins* produced by bacteria can cause serious illness.

trade wind A planetary wind that blows from east to west toward the equator. (E54) South of the equator, the *trade wind* comes from the southeast.

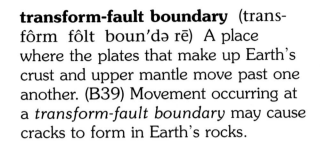

transform-fault boundary (trans-fôrm fôlt boun′də rē) A place where the plates that make up Earth's crust and upper mantle move past one another. (B39) Movement occurring at a *transform-fault boundary* may cause cracks to form in Earth's rocks.

tsunami (tso͞o nä′mē) A huge, powerful ocean wave usually caused by an underwater earthquake. (B74) A *tsunami* can cause great destruction.

turbidity current (tʉr bid′i tē kʉr′ənt) A current of water carrying large amounts of sediment. (E59) *Turbidity currents* may cause sediment to build up in some places.

upwelling The rising of deep water to the surface that occurs when winds move surface water. (E58) *Upwelling* brings pieces of shells and dead organisms up from the ocean floor.

vaccine (vak sēn′) A preparation of dead or weakened bacteria or viruses that produces immunity to a disease. (A57) The *vaccine* for smallpox has eliminated that disease.

vacuole (vak′yo͞o ōl) A structure in the cytoplasm in which food and other substances are stored. (A11) A *vacuole* in a plant cell is often quite large.

variable (ver'ē ə bəl) The one differ-ence in the setups of a controlled experiment; provides a comparison for testing a hypothesis. (S7) The *variable* in an experiment with plants was the amount of water given to each plant.

vegetative propagation (vej ə tāt'iv präp ə gā'shən) A form of asexual reproduction in which a new plant develops from a part of a parent plant. (D14) Using a cutting taken from a houseplant to grow a new plant is a method of *vegetative propagation.*

velocity (və läs'ə tē) The rate of motion in a particular direction. (F21) The *velocity* was northwest at 880 km/h.

virus (vī'rəs) A tiny disease-causing agent consisting of genetic material wrapped inside a capsule of protein. (A50) *Viruses* cause such diseases as AIDS, chickenpox, and rabies.

volcano An opening in Earth's crust through which hot gases, rock frag-ments, and molten rock erupt. (B86) Lava flowed out of the *volcano.*

volume (väl'yōōm) The amount of space that matter takes up. (C11) A large fuel tank holds a greater *volume* of gasoline than a small tank.

wave The up-and-down movement of the surface of water, caused by the wind. (E63) Ocean *waves* crashed against the shoreline.

wavelength The distance between two successive waves. (E63) At the height of the storm, the waves had a *wavelength* of 10 m.

weight A measure of the force of gravity on an object. (F33) The *weight* of this package is five pounds.

westerly (wes'tər lē) A prevailing wind that blows from west to east. (E54) Ships that sailed from North America to Europe were aided by the power of the *westerlies.*

zooplankton (zō ō plaŋk'tən) The group of tiny animal-like organisms that live near the surface of the ocean. (E11) *Zooplankton* float in the sea.

zygote (zī'gōt) A fertilized egg cell. (D24) A *zygote* develops into an embryo by means of cell division.

INDEX

Pompeii, Italy, B90
Potassium chloride, E8
Pound, F34
Priestley, Joseph, C75
Producers, A18
Professional dancers, F52–F53
Properties, of matter, C48
Protease, A58
Protease inhibitor, A58
Protein, A24
Protein molecules, C90
Protists, A28, A30, A31,
    A32–A35, E45
  animal-like, A32–A33
  multicellular, A35
  plantlike, A33–A34
Protons, C71, C76–C77
Protozoan diseases, A36–A37
Protozoans, A32–A33
Pseudopods, A32
Pterosaurs, D59
Pueblo pottery, C30
Pull, F33
Punnett square, D43
Purity, of matter, C15
Push, F33
P waves, earthquake, B65

Q
Quaternary Period, D59

R
Rabies, A51
Radiation, C77
Radioactive elements, C76
Radioactivity, C75, C76
Radon, B59
Rafinesque, Constantine
    Samuel, D64
Rance Tidal Power Station,
    France, E85
Reaction force, F90
Reactions, chemical, C70
Reaction time, in braking,
    F25–F26
Recessive gene, D38–D39,
    D40

Recessive trait, D43
Recipient, A24
Red precipitate, C39
Red Sea, E9
Reproduction, D4, D6
  by budding, D13
  by fission, D10–D12
  See also Asexual
    reproduction; Sexual
    reproduction; Vegetative
    propagation.
Research biologist, A44
Resin, D55
Reverse fault, B62
Rhizoids, A41
Rhizopus, A41
Richter, Charles, B57
Richter scale, B54, B55,
    B56–B58
Rifting and rifts, B106–B108
Rigolly, Louis, F15
Ring of Fire, B85, B94
Rios, Petrona, C62
River, The (Paulsen), F74
Robots, investigating
    volcanoes, B104–B105
Rocket, momentum of,
    F84–F85
Rocket launch, F116–F117
Rock record, B10
Roher, Heinrich, A13
Roll Back Malaria (RBM), A36
Royal Society of London, E44
Ruska, Ernst, A13
Ruthenium, C35

S
Salamanders, A25
Salinity, E9
  and density, E56
Salk, Jonas, A53
Salt, compound, C83
Salter, Stephen, E83
Salter's ducks, E82–E83
San Andreas Fault, CA, B20,
    B39, B55, B56, B57
San Diego Zoo, D26

Saprophytes, A42
Sargassum, A34
Satellite navigation systems, E45
Satellite positioning, E43
Saturn 5 rocket, F116–F117
Scale, F33
Scanning electron microscope
    (SEM), A13
Scanning tunneling microscope
    (STM), A13
Scheele, Karl Wilhelm, C75
Schleiden, Matthias, A12
Schwann, Theodor, A12
Scientific Methods ("Think Like
    a Scientist"), S2–S11
  controlled experiment, S7
  hypothesis, S6
  theory, S9
  variable, S7
Scotia Plate, B20
Scott, David Randolph, F47
Scuba, F124
Sea Cliff, DSV, B102
Sea floor
  earthquakes on, B74–B76
  magnetism, B27
  mapping, B24–B25
  spreading, B27–B28, B106
  See also Ocean floor.
Sea iguanas, D67
Seamounts, B101, B102,
    E32, E34–E35
Sea rockets, B89
Seat belts, F60–F61
Seaweed, E79
Sediments, organic, E37
Seismic waves, B72
Seismograph, B66, B72–B73
Seismologist, B50, B57
Seismometers, B96, B102
Selective breeding, D68–D69
Self-contained underwater
    breathing apparatus. *See*
    Scuba.
Sex cells, D22
Sexual reproduction, D18,
    D22–D24, D74

Underwater exploration, E42–E43
Underwater housing, E46
Upper mantle, Earth's, B19
Upwelling, E58
Uranium, C76
U.S. Geological Survey, B58

V
Vaccine, A57
Vacuoles, A7*, A11, A33
Vegetative propagation, D14–D17
Velocity, F21
  and momentum, F84
Verne, Jules, E42
Vertebrates, D64
Viral diseases, A50
  chart of, A57
Virchow, Rudolf, A13
Virgil, B104
Viruses, A50–A51
Vitamin C, C89
Volcanic eruptions
  risk of, B103
  selected (chart), B83
Volcanic island, E33
Volcanic vent, B46, B84, B88
Volcanism, and plate tectonics, B85
Volcanoes, B16, B46, B84–B91
  classifying, B86
  locating, B82
  on ocean floor, E36–E37
  worldwide, B18
Volcanoes and Earthquakes (Booth), B28, B44
Volcanologists, B90
Volume, F34–F35
  measuring, C11–C12
Volvox, A34

W
Wagstaff, Patty, F28
Walsh, Don, E18–E19, E20
Wasatch Range, UT, B45

Waste material, A17
Water
  density of, E56
  particle motion, E63
  states of, C25, C27
Water displacement, C12
Water strider, C58
Wavelength, ocean, E63
Waves, ocean, E63–E64
  dangers of, E65
Weather satellites, B96–B97
Wegener, Alfred, B6
  and drifting continents, B8–B15
Weight, F33–F34
  defined, C10
Westerlies, E54
Whaling, international ban on, E81
What Makes You What You Are: A First Look at Genetics (Bornstein), D12, D41
Wheel(s), F24
  development of, F96–F98
  early use of, F96
Whitecap, E64
Why Did the Dinosaurs Disappear? (Whitfield), D65
Width, C12
Wilcox, Howard, E84
Williams, Daniel Hale, A50, A52
Wind, E50
Wind energy, C85
Wind tunnel, F110–F111
Wong-Staal, Flossie, A44
Wood's metal, C60
World geography
  today, B15
  65 million years ago, B14
  135 million years ago, B13
  180 million years ago, B12
World Health Organization, A36
Wright, Jane, A53

Wright, Orville and Wilbur, F107
The Wright Brothers: How They Invented the Airplane (Freedman), F110

X
Xenon, C35

Y
Yeasts, A28, A40, D8–D9
Yeast bud, D13

Z
Zooplankton, E11, E24, E58
Zygote, D20*–D21, D24

* **Activity**

H45

CREDITS